HOW SALESMEN
MAKE THINGS
HAPPEN

The Magic Question Technique
That Clinches Sales Fast

HOW SALESMEN
MAKE THINGS HAPPEN

The Magic Question Technique
That Clinches Sales Fast

William Wachs

Parker Publishing Company, Inc.   West Nyack, New York

Library of Congress Cataloging in Publication Data

Wachs, William.
   How salesmen make things happen.

   1. Salesmen and salesmanship. I. Title.
HF5438.W215   658.85   72-7445
ISBN 0-13-431254-6

BY THE SAME AUTHOR:

How Sales Managers Get Things Done
The Successful Manager's Guide

How This Book Will
Make Things
Happen for You

This book deals with making things happen for salesmen because:

  ... Salesmen *have to* make things happen.

  ... There are many ways to accomplish this which the salesman may have been too busy to learn about.

Written for the salesman who is looking for specific, advanced techniques for getting better results from his time and efforts, this book illustrates:

     ... A very effective, yet little-known technique for closing sales fast.

     ... How you can capitalize on practical psychology and logic in your closing.

     ... The important role of goals in your success in closing.

     ... How you can capitalize on practical psychology and logic in your make-happen, closing-oriented presentations.

     ... The all-important part played by semantics in getting your prospect to agree with you.

     .. The magic of questions in overcoming objections.

Practical and down-to-earth, with large numbers of specific techniques for every concept discussed, this book is based on the philosophy that a salesman *can* and *must* make things happen by controlling his sales calls and his prospect's decisions to buy.

The unique features that make the book special are:

... Emphasis on the practical and a minimum of theorizing.
... Hundreds of tools and specific techniques for immediate make-happen use.
... Liberal interspersing of illustrative cases from the author's broad experience.
... Practical, easy applications of all principles to a wide variety of sales situations.

The reader's use of the ideas and systems in this book will enable him to sell more effectively and increase his income. It will arm him with a large number of specific techniques for making things happen.

William Wachs

Contents

How This Book Will Make Things Happen for You—7

Chapter 1

How the Little-Known Magic Question Technique Will Close Sales for You—15

Why Questions Hasten Closes (16)
A Winner (17)
Why Make-Happen Questions Are Superior to Statements (18)
A Personal Experience (19)
How Magic Questions Guide You to the Development of the Call (21)
Involving the Prospect Through Questions (23)
How Magic Questions Get the Prospect to Sell Himself (25)
A Definite Closing Effort vs. Continuing Closing Efforts (27)
What's a Make-Happen Close? (33)
Why You Should Be Using the Make-Happen Magic Question Technique (35)
Summary (37)

Chapter 2

How to Get Yourself Ready to Make Things Happen with Close-Clinching Sales Questions—39

How to Get Ready (40)
Preparing the Magic Make-Happen Questions (47)
Final Steps in Getting Ready (51)
Another Case (51)
Percy's Planning (52)
Summary (60)

Chapter 3

How to Use Your Sales Goals in Designing Persuasive Questions—61

Ultimate Objective of All Selling (62)
Objective for Any One Call (63)
Relationship Between Objective and Close (64)
Designing Questions for Goals (67)
Summary (86)

Chapter 4

How to Use Make-Happen Questions for Keeping the Customer Interested—87

Attention (88)
Interest (89)
Capturing Attention (89)
Introduction (90)
Recommended Openers (90)
Capturing Attention (101)
Now You Must Say or Do Something to Get Him to Turn His
        Complete Attention to What You Want to Develop (102)
Summary (111)

Chapter 5

How to Use Practical Psychology in the Magic Sales Question Technique—113

Terms (114)
Role of Psychology in Selling (116)
How Valid Psychological Principles Arise (117)
Psychology and Selling (118)
The Psychology of Presentation (122)
The Psychology of Proof (133)
The Psychology of the Make-Happen Close (134)
The Psychology of Handling Objections (135)
Psychology of the Follow-Up (136)
Summary (137)

Chapter 6

How to Use Practical Logic in the Magic Sales Question Technique—139

Making Things Happen with Facts **(140)**
Proving Facts **(141)**
Reasoning and Logic **(144)**
How to Use Logic and Questions Effectively **(146)**
Further Examples **(150)**
Summary **(162)**

Chapter 7

How to Use Semantics in the Magic Sales Question Technique—163

How to Become a Make-Happen Semanticist **(164)**
Magic Questions as an Assurance of Semantic Accuracy **(165)**
Examples of Key Words Requiring Semantic Care **(167)**
An Experience **(171)**
Back to Our Examples **(172)**
Another Experience **(174)**
A Few More Semantic Problems **(175)**
Summary **(179)**

Chapter 8

How to Make Things Happen on Actual Calls with the Magic Question Technique—181

Review of the Magic **(182)**
Beginning to Close **(184)**
Alertness to Signals **(185)**
Questions as Signal-Alerters and Close-Expediters **(185)**
Make-Happen Questions and the Close **(186)**
Finalizing Statements/Actions **(188)**
Real-Life Examples **(190)**
Summary **(202)**

Chapter 9

**How to Handle Difficult Objections Boldly and Go in for a Sure
Close with Effective Make-Happen Questions—203**

What Is an Objection? **(204)**
When and Why an Objection Is Raised **(204)**
How to Anticipate and Avoid Objections **(205)**
The Question Technique as an Objection-Avoider **(207)**
Handling Objections **(207)**
Meeting the Real McCoy **(209)**
Examples **(210)**
Objections and the Make-Happen Close **(216)**
Examples **(218)**
Summary **(224)**

Index—225

HOW SALESMEN
MAKE THINGS
HAPPEN

The Magic Question Technique
That Clinches Sales Fast

CHAPTER 1

How the Little-Known Magic Question Technique Will Close Sales for You

Close sales—that's what every professional salesman wants to do. And the more closes, the merrier.

There are many ways to approach this goal, but there's one sure-fire method to make the close happen: ask the right questions, at the right times—and act wisely on the answers you get.

Sounds simple, and it is simple—and this book will show you in step-by-step detail how you can take advantage of this little-used magic question technique for closing a maximum number of meaningful sales in the shortest time possible.

WHY QUESTIONS HASTEN CLOSES

To see how you can start asking make-happen questions right away, let's first analyze what actually goes into the decision of your prospect to go along with your close.

- He needs, wants and/or feels the lack of something which you have to offer.
- He may not be completely aware or convinced that what you're selling is exactly what he should buy—at least, from you.
- Before he decides to accept *your* offer he must:

    —Really listen to what you are saying.
    —Fully understand everything you present to him.
    —Agree with your conviction that it is exactly what he should have.

Some salesmen ask questions only to get the prospect to agree with a statement that the salesman has made. Let's see what the weaknesses of this approach are, as contrasted with the strengths of the Make-Happen Magic Question Technique.

Parallel Case Studies

Harry Nabors sells an industrial thread used by a swimsuit manufacturer.

I went out with Harry on a number of calls. After the preliminaries, he went right into his pitch. He developed the following points without pause or interruption:

1. Our industrial thread is the best for swimsuits.
2. We have a larger thread-color selection than any other company in the same business.
3. Our thread has the lowest shrinkage factor in the product field.
4. We stock our products close enough to your factory to give you fast and reliable service.

Now, everything that Nabors said was true, but I would watch the prospect's face as the salesman talked. More often than not the buyer wasn't really listening—although he pretended to—and Harry never stopped to find out the extent of receptivity of the other man.

When my companion finished his spiel, the prospect would generally either:

- Say he'd let him know.
- Ask him to leave samples and literature.
- Raise insurmountable objections.
- Turn Harry down, point-blank.

A WINNER

Now let's see how Phil Mabey does it. He sells a service—the facilities of his hotel for conventions and other meetings. Here's how Phil begins his presentation:

I don't want to take up your time unless I'm convinced that what I have to offer is of real benefit to you. That's why I'd like to ask you some questions.

—When is your next convention?
—How many people do you expect to attend?
—How many days will it last?
—About how many rooms will you need for your participants?
—What meals and beverage services will you require?
—What quality standards have you set for the service you want?
—What is your budget for the convention?

When Phil had the answers to these questions, he was able to demonstrate how his hotel could meet those requirements better than any other facility. He usually came away with a commitment.

WHY MAKE-HAPPEN QUESTIONS ARE SUPERIOR TO STATEMENTS

When you sit down with a prospect, you generally want to get him to commit himself to a statement or action which he hadn't decided on before your call. But it's important first to find out whether you're really barking up the right tree before you spend too much time with him, only to discover that he wasn't a valid prospect at all—at least, not for that offer on that occasion.

Suppose he was properly qualified before you approached him. That's not enough. All kinds of factors can arise which make him not interested in buying that day.

Since your time is valuable—the more closes, the more sales—you don't want to stay any longer with any one prospect, unless the certainty of a close warrants it.

Thus, in every case, your first obligation—to yourself as well as to your prospect—is to make every minute count. Here is the sequence of make-happen ideas involved in the first phase of the interview:

1. You have done as much qualifying as you could of the prospect, before you called on him.
2. You have a specific goal for that interview.
3. You want to spend all the time with him that is essential for the achievement of your reason for seeing him that day.
4. You don't want to stay there during any period of time when he has already decided that he won't commit himself—at least that day—to what you want him to do or say.
5. You want to be sure to recognize any signals that he might be putting out to the effect that you're really wasting your time during that interview.
6. You want to be sure that you're on the right track, or that it would be better to change objectives or plan to come back some other time when your efforts would be more productive.
7. There is no more effective way of accomplishing all of this than the proper use of make-happen questions.

An Example

Let's take the situation I observed on a joint call with Oswald Johnson.

He was calling on the construction engineer of a company which was planning a new plant. Os wanted to get the prospect to use his company's pre-fabricated partitions wherever separation of people was desirable without going into fully enclosed rooms. He had found out everything he could about the prospect, before going there, and had reason to believe that a visit on that day was worth the time and effort.

Here's the conversation that took place after the opening moments of the call:

> *Os:*   Mr. Laban, I'd like to make sure that I make your time with me the most valuable to you, so I'm going to ask you some questions. About how many partitions do your plans call for?
>
> *Laban:*   About 30.
>
> *Os:*   What are the average dimensions of the partitions you plan?
>
> *Laban:*   Six feet high by eight by eight.
>
> *Os:*   What kinds of materials have you planned on using for your partitions?
>
> *Laban:*   We haven't gotten that far yet.

At this point Os realized that his original objective would be unachievable during that call. Having anticipated that possibility, he was prepared with an alternative goal, and went on as follows:

> *Os:*   When will you be investigating the specs?
>
> *Laban:*   We'll be starting to do that in about two weeks.

Os then proceeded to try to sell Laban on letting Os come and see him the following week to give him the benefit of Os' and his company's broad experience in writing specs for the kinds of partitions Laban needed.

Because Os asked the right kinds of questions—the *magic* kinds of questions—he realized early in the interview that his original objective was wrong, switched at once to an achievable goal and succeeded in getting the appointment he wanted.

Os had won the prospect's confidence by not trying to close for an order when that was not the appropriate goal. He was able, on the next call, to convince his prospect that his suggested specs for the partitions were exactly what the company needed for its new plant. Os got an order for the whole job. And that's how he made things happen.

A PERSONAL EXPERIENCE

Many years ago, I was the Sales Manager for a company that sold sales consulting services. I also served as the Chief Sales Consultant to our clients.

One of my men had uncovered a real, live prospect: the Sales Manager of a large company who was looking for an outside consultant to conduct a sales-training program for his 15 salesmen, all operating in one city. My man had asked me to help him close the sale because the prospect wanted to meet the consultant—me—who would administer the sessions before engaging us.

An appointment was made for the sales call and my man briefed me in advance on the situation. The main consideration was that the prospect wanted a tailored program for just his problems, not a packaged setup.

Here's the conversation that took place between him and me:

Prospect: Well, what can you do for me?

W.W.: I don't know yet. I'll have to ask you a few questions first. How many salesmen will be present during each session?

Prospect: All fifteen.

W.W.: How many sessions are you allowing for?

Prospect: I have to have the program finished in one month.

W.W.: How many hours can you let me have for each session?

Prospect: As many as you can keep the men awake for after work.

W.W.: Do you have a list of the subjects you want taken up or is that something still to be developed?

Prospect: All I care about is that it shouldn't be a canned program. I want training tailored to the specific requirements for selling my products in the most profitable way possible. Now, how will you go about training my men if I give you the job?

W.W.: I haven't the slightest idea.

Prospect: What do you mean? I thought you were an expert.

W.W.: You said that you wanted the program tailored to your specific needs. I can't tell you at this point what kind of program we can offer. I'll have to make a survey of your sales force, your objectives for them and the problems you and your men are having. Only then will I be in a position to tell you how I would train them for greater effectiveness.

At this point the prospect said: "You're on! I've interviewed half a dozen consultants. You're the first one who gave me the answer I've been looking for."

It's true that I didn't close the consulting-training sale that day. But my questions had confirmed what my salesman had told me. The prospect wasn't *ready* to buy a training program. So I took advantage of the signals his answers afforded me, switched objectives and closed on a survey. Once I'd completed that, it was easy to make things happen and get the order for the training program—and it was a great success.

An Anecdote

No treatment of the importance of probing the prospect before going too far would be complete without that old chestnut of the vacuum-cleaner salesman.

When the lady of the house opened the door slightly, his foot immediately went in far enough to assure her inability to close the door. When he told her he had the most marvelous vacuum cleaner in the world, she told him she wasn't interested. Nevertheless, he worked his way into the living room, talking all the while.

Suddenly, he took out a large bag of refuse and spilled it on the carpet. In horror, she asked him what he was doing. Here's the rest of the chatter that took place:

He: I'm going to demonstrate how marvelous this machine is. I'll pick up all this refuse in no time flat, and anything that's left I'll eat.

She: Will you excuse me for a moment?

He: Where are you going?

She: To the kitchen to get some ketchup and salt. Our electric current has been closed off this afternoon for repairs to one of the lines.

HOW MAGIC QUESTIONS GUIDE YOU TO THE DEVELOPMENT OF THE CALL

Now let's assume that your questions have revealed that you're on the right path toward achieving your objective for the visit. The next thing you make happen is to reason with the prospect in the most logical and chronological way possible. I'll be going into greater detail later on the role of logic and chronology in a sales interview, but now I want to limit myself to the help you can get from questions in making the best kind of presentation.

Here's the problem I'm talking about:

- You want to close on whatever your objective is for that call.
- You know that you stand a good chance of achieving your goal.
- The task is, however, not going to be easy.
- The prospect must understand each step of the development of your reasoning before he is convinced that he should go along with what you are offering him.

Now, if he loses interest somewhere along the way, he may be too polite to interrupt you. With the right kinds of make-happen questions you can:

—Make sure that he is really listening and fully understands each step of the development.

—Select the best points to make next, in the light of his answers, in order to arrive at the conclusion you desire.

—Bring him to the stage where he is with you 100%, as you go from one phase to another of your sequence of ideas.

An Illustration

Let's take the sales call that Rudy Quadrell made one day. He sold advertising time for a television station and had established satisfactorily that the prospect was interested in spending a portion of his advertising budget on that medium. Rudy's goal was to get the prospect to make a firm commitment, that day, to as profitable a time schedule as possible.

Rudy didn't, however, know just what that budget was. He was also ignorant of several other facts essential for him to determine the best line to follow in trying to close to the greatest mutual benefit of the prospect and himself. Here was how Rudy effectively used questions to make sure he kept constantly on the right track:

Rudy:　　Now that we've agreed that television advertising plays an important role in your overall marketing effort, I'm eager to help you decide how to make the most profitable use of that medium. Approximately how many people do you expect to reach with your message in all the media you employ?

Prospect:　　Around 100,000.

Rudy:　　What do you figure your cost per 1,000 reached to be?

Prospect:　　Around $100.

Rudy:　　What is it costing you to reach 1,000 people through your newspaper advertising?

Prospect:　　About that figure, $100.

Rudy: Does your advertising budget cover all the people you want to reach through the newspapers, or do you still miss substantial prospects because of the high proportionate costs?

Prospect: I can't afford to spend all the money I need to cover my whole potential market just through newspaper advertising.

Rudy was then confident that his prospect was ready to be convinced that the cost per 1,000 reached was lower through his television advertising package, and was able to work out a schedule of allocation of budget between the two media. By the use of magic questions, he brought both himself and the prospect to the right line of reasoning, which led to the ultimate close.

Another Example

Sandy Kaback sold a process for accelerating the ripening of bananas in warehouses. Sandy was calling on the Produce Merchandiser of a warehouse and had established that he was not satisfied with the length of time it took to move the bananas from receipt into the warehouse to the consumer. Sandy asked the following questions:

1. Why do you have to keep the bananas in the warehouse that long? (To ripen sufficiently.)
2. What process are you now using? (Just keep the warehouse at the right temperature.)
3. How much do you calculate it's costing you for each day of ripening for a warehouseful? ($5,000.)

Sandy felt that his prospect was now ready to understand and accept the fact that:

- His company's humidity-ripening process was quicker than, and in all respects superior to, the one currently being used by the prospect.
- The cost of buying his company's process was far less per warehouseful of bananas than the loss in revenue due to slower turnover.

The answers to the questions he asked showed Sandy that he was still on the right track, guiding him step by step in both his questions and his proof of value to the prospect of the humidity process.

INVOLVING THE PROSPECT THROUGH QUESTIONS

Some salesmen talk and talk, hoping that the prospect will exhibit interest, listen and become convinced. These salesmen don't really know, until they try to close, whether they will succeed or not. But if the buyer participates in the reasoning that leads to a conclusion, he's more likely to accept and agree with that conclusion.

The salesman who asks his prospects the right number and kinds of magic questions, and acts appropriately on the prospects' responses, is constantly *involving* the buyer and making things happen.

A Contrast

Non-involvement

Let's take, first, an example of the salesman who does all the talking except when the prospect begins to raise objections.

Bernie Rabb, whom I accompanied one day on a call to the Director of Purchasing of a large soft-drink manufacturer, wanted to get the buyer to permit his company to test-pack the manufacturer's syrup in a fibre 1-gallon can. Bernie engaged in a monologue that went something like this:

> My company has been making a fibre 1-gallon can for the last 23 years. Our can is more rigid than the one you're now using to pack your syrup. It's better for export shipments. You can package your syrup faster in our cans than in your present container. Fibre is better than plastic, which you are now using. Our R and D Department is always at your disposal. We know what you need, and are prepared to offer you our long experience and superior packaging knowledge.

Bernie didn't get the order. As he was talking, I was watching the prospect. His face and posture revealed the following attitudes, one at a time or simultaneously:

- Indignation at the superior tone Bernie conveyed.
- Disagreement with a number of the things Bernie said.
- Boredom with the steady recital.
- Resignation that he'd never get a word in edgewise.

Involvement

Now let's convert Bernie's monologue into a make-happen dialogue and see how that would have led to an easy close, because—among other results from the proper use of questions—the prospect was and felt continually involved.

    A. What kind of container do you use to package your syrup? (One-gallon plastic.)

    B. Why do you use a plastic container? (It has a low unit cost, doesn't affect the taste too much and is readily available.)

C. What elements do you calculate in arriving at that unit cost? (Just the cost of the container.)

D. What other kinds of containers have you tried? (None.)

E. Why not? (We seem to be maximizing our profit and customer satisfaction with the container we're now using.)

F. How long will your present supply of plastic containers last? (Six months before we re-order.)

Bernie could have, at this point, capitalized on his prospect's involvement by taking up one after another of his answers to Bernie's questions, along these lines:

1. The real cost to you of the containers you use must include the time (labor) of filling and stoppering. I want to prove to you that our fibre 1-gallon can is more rapidly filled and, including the cost of the container itself, will cost you considerably less.

2. I'd like to prove to you that our fibre container doesn't affect the taste of the syrup at all.

3. We have a manufacturing plant within economical access to each of your producing establishments.

4. We have figures to show that syrup producers using our containers consistently gain and hold greater customer satisfaction. Also, we have figures which show you how our containers will definitely increase your profit picture.

5. Since you don't have to re-order for another six months, now is a good time to let us test-pack your syrup in our fibre containers. Before you have to place your order for more containers, we'll be able to prove to you that ours are. . . .

Thus you see that if Bernie had *involved* his prospect constantly, through questions, he could have assured attention, interest, understanding and receptivity. Then, by picking up each response of his prospect, he could have easily led to the close he'd been seeking all along.

HOW MAGIC QUESTIONS GET THE PROSPECT TO SELL HIMSELF

Let's now turn our attention to another—and very strong—reason why good questions facilitate and assure successful closes.

What is the selling process, really? Here's a valid analysis:

—I want to sell my products or services only to those prospects who can really benefit from what I have to offer. This is both because I'm an ethical salesman (working for an ethical company) and because I don't want to lose customers or my company's (and my own) valuable reputation for honesty.

—Through qualifying (in large measure by probing with questions during the interview), I am convinced that my product or service will really benefit the prospect.

—He may not be aware of this fact.

—If I can get *him* to tell *me* what *I* want to tell *him,* I can be sure that:

- He has paid attention to everything I've said.
- He fully understands what's involved.
- He fully accepts the fact that what I have to offer is exactly what he wants or needs.

—Therefore, the most effective way to sell is to get the prospect to convince *himself* of the validity of what I want to convince him of.

The only sure way to accomplish this is by the proper use of questions. Here are some illustrations:

1. I try to convince the prospect

Let's see what happens when I try to convince the prospect that what I have to offer is of benefit to him.

The situation involves my effort to get an order for labels on packages of cheese.

What I say	His possible reaction
My company's labels are better printed than the ones you're now using.	So what? I don't believe you. I like the way my present labels look.
My company's service to you is better and quicker than that of the company you're now using.	What else would you say? I'm entirely satisfied with my present supplier.
Our labels are of better quality.	We don't need any better quality than what we're now using.
You really should have a second source of supply.	Why? Our present supplier is thoroughly reliable. Besides, we can always get a second supplier when we need one.

2. I get the prospect to tell me what I want to tell him

What I want him to tell me	How I get him to do so
My customers' decision to buy my cheese is partly based on the overall appearance of the package.	What effect does your cheese *package* have on your customers' decision to buy?

What I want him to tell me	How I get him to do so
The label is an important part of that package.	What role does the label play in the importance of the package?
What my customers look for in the label is ready legibility, attractiveness and solid adhesiveness.	What do your customers expect from your labels?
I require from my labels ease of application, low cost and ready availability.	What do *you* require of your labels?
My present labels don't fully meet all of those requirements.	Let's analyze your present labels, spec by spec, and see to what extent they meet your requirements.

Since my labels meet his requirements better than his present labels, and he's already indicated that he's interested in something better, I need only show him how my labels are superior to make things happen.

A DEFINITE CLOSING EFFORT VS. CONTINUING CLOSING EFFORTS

The traditional approach to selling runs something like this:

- The salesman tells the prospect how the salesman's product or service will benefit the prospect.
- The prospect keeps on raising questions and/or objections, which the salesman tries to overcome, while he really loses control of the interview.
- The salesman (if he's really brave enough to do so) finally tries to close, as a separate step in the selling process.

While I don't wish to criticize this time-worn process, I do want to state that it is inferior to what I shall soon describe, because:

- —The interview becomes a series of separate steps, interrupted from time to time by detracting ideas and convictions.
- —The closing efforts don't necessarily flow directly from *all* that precedes them.
- —The closing effort has to be a distinct part of the interview, which doesn't create the desired appearance of a perfectly natural and unavoidable end to the preceding conversations and demonstrations.
- —The salesman usually doesn't know whether he's going to succeed until he tries to close, and, if he fails to close, he doesn't really know whether he should have realized his inevitable failure earlier in the conversation. Such an earlier awareness could have resulted in either a change to a more

likely-to-succeed objective or a valid decision not to persist that day with that prospect.

The Continuing-Close Concept

The Magic Question Technique will close sales for you for yet another reason: it makes the closing of a sale a continuing, natural process, requiring no extra effort and assuring success at the end.

Here's how the question technique approaches the matter of closing.

Purpose of every call

Naturally, every sales call has, as its objective, to get the prospect to make a firm commitment to do or say what the salesman wants him to during that interview. This objective is just as applicable to the closing technique to be described here as to the traditional approach to closing.

Steps in the question technique which represent continuing closing

Here is a list of the steps involved in the use of questions during a sales call, such steps representing a continuing close, illustrated by an actual case I observed recently.

Steps in assuring either a smooth, natural close or an early realization that a change in objective (or early withdrawal) is in order.	Illustration from a sales call made by Denny Sabatino on a cold cereal buyer for a super-market chain.
1. Select as the prospect for a specific call one or more people qualified, as far in advance of the call as possible, to benefit from the product or service being offered and authorized to make or contribute materially to the buying decision.	Denny had already ascertained that the man he was going to call on had the authority to place orders for cold cereal for all the stores in his chain, which already sold cold cereals from their shelves.
2. Properly go through the opening moments of the interview.	Denny introduced himself, established good rapport and captured the buyer's attention promptly.
3. State convincingly that you are interested in taking up both	Denny said: "Mr. Jones, while I'm confident that my reason for

Steps in assuring either a smooth, natural close or an early realization that a change in objective (or early withdrawal) is in order.	Illustration from a sales call made by Denny Sabatino on a cold cereal buyer for a super-market chain.
the prospect's and your own time, only if this is to the distinct advantage of both; use that approach to introduce the fact that you're going to start right in by asking questions.	being here now is to your distinct advantage, as well as mine, I want to make sure that I'm right. That's why I'd like to ask you a few questions."

Intermediate observation

At this point, I interrupt the development of the two previous columns to indicate how you should proceed throughout the entire interview in order to be most effective in using the question technique.

1. Start right in asking your questions. Remember that you ask questions even when you know the answers, in order to:

    a. Assure his continued attention and interest.
    b. Get him involved.
    c. Assure that he completely understands what you're there to communicate.
    d. Get him to tell you what you wanted to tell him.

2. During the question-asking period, don't talk about your product or service. You can ask only those questions which will lead to answers most favorable to your product or service, but limit yourself to concepts and needs without specifically mentioning what you want to sell and why it's best for him. You'll get your chance to do that later.

3. Listen very carefully to his answers and make sure you understand them exactly as he means them.

4. If his answers begin to indicate that he's really not interested (or can't benefit from your offer), try to switch your objective to something valuable in which you can succeed. If this is impossible, leave the door open for coming back some other time when you have a better chance to succeed, bow out gracefully and skedaddle to another more likely prospect.

5. If his answers reveal that you're on the right track, make sure that each next question is a direct outgrowth of his answer to your preceding question and is designed to lead him right down the primrose path of buying from you.

Now let's get back to our two-columned chart.

Steps	Illustration
4. Start to ask your questions.	a. Mr. Jones, approximately what percentage of your chain shelf space is assigned to cold cereals? b. About how many different brands and kinds of cold cereals do you carry? c. What causes you to decide on a particular brand and kind of cold cereal to stock in specific quantities?
5. Be prepared to ask questions which will elicit specs he might overlook which are most favorable to your product or service.	What importance do you give in deciding which brand and kind to stock, with regard to: a. Proven customer demand? b. Greater profitability? c. The reputation for a wide variety of brands? d. Attractive packaging? e. Good customer value? f. Ease of using the package? g. Delicious flavor? h. Greater volume per shelf footage occupied? i. Supplier advertising and promotion programs?
6. Ask any additional questions which will help advance your product or service.	a. What do you consider good delivery time? b. How often do you expect your salesmen to check up on stock in the stores? c. What kind of return policy do you look for?
7. Proceed to state how your product or service meets what he, himself, has indicated he wants, and that your *package* (your product or service, your company and you, yourself) meets his needs better than	Well, Mr. Jones, I'm very glad you've told me what you did, because what you've said you look for in cold cereals is exactly what we offer, and better than anyone else. Here, let me show you.

Steps	Illustration
any other combination of factors in the competition. Prove each statement calling for or requiring proof.	a. You said that one of your reasons for deciding on the cold cereals you buy is proven customer demand. Here's a survey we've just completed which proves that 23% of all cold cereals bought, in stores which carry our brand as well as others, are ours. b. You quite properly placed great emphasis on the profitability of a cold cereal in determining whether you'd stock it. Here is a comparative study we make each year, the current one showing that we rank second in profitability of all competitive cold cereals. The first is a brand that we agree everyone must carry, but it sells only 40% of the total cold cereal market. c. Ours is a prestige brand, as proven by these poll results, which adds to a store's reputation for wide varieties of stocking. d. Compare the packaging of our cold cereals with that of the competitive brands and you'll see why we've won these packaging awards reported in this magazine. e. Compare the cost per ounce of our cereal to that of the competition, as revealed in this report, and you'll see why purchasers of our cereal feel so good about the value the store gives them for their money. f. Let me demonstrate how much easier it is to use our

Steps	Illustration
	package than those of the competition, and you'll see why these testimonials are so freely given to us.
	g. I'd like you to taste this cereal right now, so you can better understand why your customers will appreciate your stocking it for them.
	h. Compare the weight of the contents of this box to the space it occupies on the shelf and you'll see why it represents greater profitability per shelf foot.
	i. I'm glad you mentioned the importance to your buying decision of supplier advertising and promotion. Let me show you how extensive and effective our program is. Here are the ads we plan to place in the next six months, and here are the promotion materials we make available to you. Your own judgment of their attractiveness and pull will be substantiated by these figures, validated by the XYZ Poll Company.
8. Assume that you have closed the sale and make a statement (or ask a question) which will get the buyer to commit himself then and there to what you want.	Either: a. Our experience has proven that for a chain like yours an initial order of 20,000 boxes is the most profitable. I've put that amount down on this order form and would appreciate your reviewing it before you sign it.

Steps	Illustration
	Or: b. Would you prefer to place an order now for immediate delivery to your warehouses of 20,000 boxes, or would you rather have us hold 10,000 for you on a firm order for next month, shipping the first 10,000 right away?
9. If he raises objections, obstacles or questions, handle them and move right in on the close again.	(See the chapter, following, on the use of questions in handling objections.)
10. Don't stop trying until you get a firm commitment from him for what you wanted him to do or say. Once you get a firm order, thank him, make arrangements for appropriate follow-up and leave at once.	

WHAT'S A MAKE-HAPPEN CLOSE?

Up to now I've been using, as examples of the application of the question technique, only calls leading to getting an order at the end of the interview. Later on in the book, I will use other situations as well. But, in order to demonstrate now that the technique is applicable to all kinds of objectives and closes, I'll take a situation that doesn't call for trying to get an order at the end of the visit.

I was out with Leonard Waddell one day. He was a salesman for a company that warehoused and fabricated steel for the ultimate user. The man he was to see was the Manufacturing Manager of a company that made snowmobiles.

The customer had ordered 500 tons of a particular grade of steel to be cut and shaped according to his specifications. The steel had been shipped and the customer invoiced.

When the normal period for payment (including statements of payments due) had come and gone, without a check, the Credit Department asked the Sales Manager whether he wanted to look into the matter before pressure was brought to bear on the customer. Since the latter had always been a good source of profitable business, and prompt in his payments, the Sales Manager decided to take the Credit Manager up on his suggestion.

The account belonged to Leonard. He planned to stop in and see him on a day when I was making joint calls with him.

Here's how Leonard used the make-happen question technique in this situation, which was *not* a call designed to get an order.

Call objective:	To find out why the customer didn't pay the invoice, do everything possible to overcome any customer dissatisfaction that might exist, keep the customer satisfied with the company's continued ability to sell him to his advantage and get the customer to send a check.
Questions asked:	1. Mr. Jones, do you have our latest invoice handy or would you like to see my copy? 2. Would you care to tell me why it hasn't been paid yet?
Jones' reply:	Yes, I'll tell you! Everything that could have gone wrong with that shipment did. Instead of 500 tons I received 476 tons, but I was billed for 500. Fourteen of the plates were too short. And to top it off, the shipment arrived two days late and had been improperly loaded on your trailer. It cost me more money to unload it than the profit I can make on the parts represented by your steel.
Leonard:	Mr. Jones, why didn't you phone me right away, or tell me about it when I followed up last month on the sale we're talking about?
Jones:	Because I was hopping mad—that's why! I figured you'd given me a hard time, so I'd give you a hard time and keep you guessing.
Leonard:	Mr. Jones, how many years have you been buying steel from me? (Five years.) And how many times have you had cause to be dissatisfied with our product or service?
Jones:	Well, this is the first time, it's true, but the goof was so awful, and it came at a time when I was very busy, so I got good and sore.

Leonard: Nor do I blame you, but let's see what we can do about rectifying the situation and restoring our regular, good, mutually beneficial relationship.

(Leonard has just begun the transition into the *close* of the visit in order to achieve his objectives for the call.)

I've made note of everything you've told me and am going right back to the plant to see how we can straighten this whole thing out. When can I phone you tomorrow to let you know how we're going to adjust the situation?

How soon after that will you be able to send us a check for the adjusted amount?

When will it be convenient for you to receive the additional steel?

What were the details of the incorrect loading?

When will you be ready to place your next order?

What day will be better for me to come by, March 15th or March 20th?

Final close: 1. Is there anything else that I can do to re-establish our normal, good relationship, or can I assume that you're entirely satisfied that we'll do right by you?

2. What can I do in the future to prevent this sort of misunderstanding from reaching those proportions?

3. Well, then, thank you for being so cooperative. I assure you that this whole matter will be settled to your complete satisfaction and that this sort of thing won't happen again. I'll see you on the 20th and I'll have my order book ready. So long!

WHY YOU SHOULD BE USING THE MAKE-HAPPEN MAGIC QUESTION TECHNIQUE

1. The question technique will lead to far more numerous and profitable closes than the traditional statement approach. You, therefore, can't afford to fail to use it effectively.
2. If you establish the right kind of rapport with your prospects they'll be receptive to anything you say and do, within reason. And if you don't establish rapport with them, even the statement technique won't work. The only difference is that you won't know you've failed until you've wasted a lot of time with them, nor will you know why you've failed.
3. When you ask questions, you should do so with the proper intonation and expression. Present a demeanor of mingled respect for the prospect, confidence in your "package," humility and a sincere desire to know.

4. Most people like to be asked their opinions. Your prospects are no exception to this. When you ask them questions, you give *them* a chance to shine. They'll love it.

5. When you know the answer to a question, you can always soften the inquiry by saying something like: "I'm not sure. What's the...?" or, "Would you confirm my understanding? How ...?" But remember: you're better off if he tells you what you wanted to tell him.

6. If you begin to feel that you're asking too many questions in a row, interpolate a few statements, but don't let this interfere with the proper development of your ideas.

Summary

1. If, when you reach the end of a sales call, you fail to close, you may have wasted a lot of time. There were probably many signals floating about to show you that you were on the wrong track, but you didn't spot them. If you rely largely on questions, in your presentation, you'll catch every signal as it comes up, and either:
   a. Use it as a springboard for switching your objective and questions before you waste any time? or
   b. Realize that there's no point in spending any more time that day with that prospect, thus making it possible for you to devote yourself to more likely prospects.

2. The same questions which might reveal to you that you're on the wrong track serve also to advance the development of your offer if it turns out that you're on the *right* track. Thus, all you have to do is ask *one* set of questions. If they are properly framed and asked, they will either guide you to a change in plan or lead you right to a successful close.

3. Questions assure prospect attention, interest, understanding and receptivity.

4. The prospect's answers to your questions guide you to the best points to make and the most effective sequence of such points.

5. By getting the prospect to answer your questions, you bring him along, step by step, in the direction toward which *you* want him to go.

6. By getting the prospect to answer your questions, you *involve* him in the interview and he's more inclined to go along with your proposition.

7. The proper kinds and sequence of questions get the prospect to *sell himself* on your proposition, thus leading him easily and naturally to the close you want.

8. The question technique makes the *whole interview* one continuous close. There's no need to introduce an artificial closing effort at the end. His answers will either reveal—early in the interview—that you should change your tactics, or they will lead you smoothly to the point where you have to do nothing more than assume that you've succeeded and generally turn out to be right. And if your assumption is incorrect, you'll know that somewhere along the line you've failed to ask the right question or react properly to his answer.

9. When you ask your questions, talk about *his* needs—*not* your product or service. Of course, your questions must be framed in such a way that if you are right about his being able to benefit from your offer, his answers will definitely lend themselves to that conclusion.

10. When you've asked all the questions you should, and he's answered them, all you have to do is show him how what you have to offer is exactly what *he, himself,* said he wanted.

11. Then move in at once on the close, and after he has raised an objection which you've successfully handled, close again.

12. Establish the right rapport with your prospect and he'll go along with you in your use of this technique. And you'll make things *happen* in selling!

CHAPTER 2

How to Get Yourself Ready to Make Things Happen with Close-Clinching Sales Questions

This chapter shows *how* to get yourself ready to make things happen through questions, *how* to plan your sales calls for guaranteed successful closes.

The evening before you plan to call on any one prospect you must start getting ready to ask him the right questions. It won't take you very much time each evening to get ready; these are simple but proven make-happen planning techniques.

As to calls you make during the day which you either didn't expect to make or weren't sure you'd make, here are my suggestions:

—If there's any chance at all that you might call on a particular prospect the next day, get ready for him anyway. You can always use the same plan when you do call on him.

—If you had absolutely no way of anticipating the night before that you'd call on him today, at least try to do some thinking before you go in to see him. But don't worry about this too much, because with a little practice, you'll be able to use questions effectively in an emergency which just didn't allow time for planning.

HOW TO GET READY

Examine Previous Records

The first step in any effective planning of sales calls is to review all relevant information about the prospect/customer. Let me clarify, at this point, some of the terms I use:

- If you expect to see a potential buyer for the first time (and he's never bought anything at all from your company), he's a *prospect*.
- If he's already bought something from your company, he's a *customer*—but:

   —Every customer must be considered a *prospect* for more or different business.

40

—You must always be alert to *sell* more or different business whenever you go to see either a customer or a prospect, regardless of your reason for seeing him *that* day.

• If this is the first time that you (or anyone else in your company) will be visiting that prospect, you'd better have at least *some* information about him before you decide to call on him.

A. If at all possible, you should have *qualified* him for the wisdom of spending your time with him.
   (i)   What is the potential volume of business you can get from him? There are many directories and other sources of information you can use for this.
   (ii) Which of your products or services are most likely to be of benefit to him?
   (iii) Who is (are) the decision-maker(s)?
   (iv) When is the best time to see him (them)?
   (v)   Are there any credit matters you should look into first?

B. If you just can't get this kind of information about the prospect in advance, your decision to call on him on any one day should be guided by the following considerations:
   (i)   You're going to see him primarily to *probe,* in order to determine the amount of time and attention he warrants.
   (ii) You'll equate the time you need for that probing with the disposition of your time for prospects/customers about whom you do have adequate information.

What Material You Review

So now you're ready to study all available information on the prospect. Depending on the situation you find yourself in, select your sources from the following checklist:

1. Your card or file on prospects/customers, showing at least the following information:
   • Company (or individual) name, address, telephone number and how to get there.
   • Nature of the business in which they are engaged.
   • Products/services (among those you have to offer) which they could buy from you, which (if any) they're buying from your competition (and why) and the potential volume of their purchases from you.
   • The best person(s) to contact; when, where and how; any information available on how best to approach him (them).
   • Credit information (as relevant).

2. Any relevant records of contacts with that prospect by others in your company.

3. Your own records of previous visits to him.

First Decision

Now you're ready to do your active planning. The very first step in this getting-ready process is to decide *why* you want to see that particular prospect at that particular time. In a later chapter, I shall go into this question of goals in considerable detail, but I'd like to explain here, briefly, what I mean.

We all know that the *ultimate* objective of *every* sales call is a closed sale. Now, if your product/service lends itself to your ability (and goal) to come away *from each call* with a firm order or commitment, then by all means make that the objective for each call.

In many businesses, however, it's impossible to get a firm order on each interview, no matter how successful the salesman. There are certain steps which simply must be taken, each on a different visit, before you make things happen with a firm order.

Therefore, before you go to see any prospect, you must first think through carefully which of the many possible reasons you can have for seeing him, and then set up that particular reason as your goal for the next day's call on him.

An Illustrative Case

As I go through the getting-ready process with you in this chapter, I'll use as an example the case of a salesman I once guided in preparing make-happen questions, and with whom I went out for a week of calls.

On Thursday evening of a particular week, I was working with the man, Cy Vaccaro, on his plans for calling on an O.E.M. the next day. The company involved made, among other things, small processing machines requiring—along with everything else—aluminum castings.

Cy reviewed the following facts:

- Sometimes the company made its own castings and other times it bought them from outside suppliers.
- The volume of such castings justified the visit.
- Cy's company had never yet approached the O.E.M. for any reason at all, but it was a solid organization and worth acquiring as a customer.
- The right man to see was the company's Castings Buyer, and he was available at 10 a.m. the next day.

Cy was now ready to write down the thoughts he would think through in his planning.

A Planning Form

Now, before continuing with that case, here's a form that I've devised for use in getting ready for asking make-happen questions.

Worksheet for Getting Ready to Close Through Sales Questions		
Date of planned call . . . . Time		
Company/individual prospect		
Address		
How to get there		
People to see		Position or title
Objective for the visit		
My first thinking on what message I'd like to get across to him (them) during the call.	A more logical/ chronological arrangement of those ideas.	Questions I would like to ask to help me elicit some of those ideas from him (them).

Back to Our Case

Now let's return to how Cy and I started to plan for the next day's call. We took a copy of the form just described and began to fill in the top portion as follows:

Date: March 17, 19___ **Time:** From 10:00 a.m. to about 11:00 a.m.
Prospect: XYZ Manufacturing Co.
Address . . . .
How to get there . . . .
Person to see: Jack Jones, Castings Buyer.

Now we had to decide on the objective for the call. Cy knew that it was general industry practice in his kind of business for the supplier who desired to sell castings to that kind of O.E.M. to quote on the job first. His quote would then be considered along with those made by the competition before a buying decision was made.

Cy therefore put down as his:

Objective for To get the Castings Buyer's authorization to submit a
the visit: quote for aluminum castings for the machine in
                   question.

First thinking

Now we were ready to fill in the first vertical column on the form:

My first thinking on what message I'd like to get across to him during the call.

As you get ready for tomorrow's session, start to think of the ideas you'd like to get across to the prospect at that time, no matter how those thoughts come to mind. As you get an idea, write it down at once in the next available full space in your column on the form.

Here's an example of how Cy filled in that first column.

My first thinking on what message I'd like to get across to him during the call.	
1. Our aluminum castings are just what you need. 2. We want to quote on supplying you with castings for your ABC machine.	

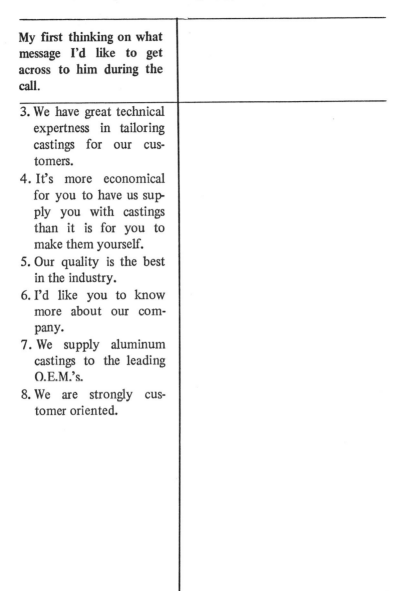

My first thinking on what message I'd like to get across to him during the call.	
3. We have great technical expertness in tailoring castings for our customers.	
4. It's more economical for you to have us supply you with castings than it is for you to make them yourself.	
5. Our quality is the best in the industry.	
6. I'd like you to know more about our company.	
7. We supply aluminum castings to the leading O.E.M.'s.	
8. We are strongly customer oriented.	

The next step in the planning

Now Cy was ready to fill in the second column. I had already trained him in the know-how. His requirement was, now, to take the statements he'd put down in the first column and re-arrange them in a more logical/chronological sequence in the second column, making sure to delete any unimportant items and add any important ones which he had overlooked in his first thinking.

Here's how Cy filled in the second column, with my help. As you read this, refer to the first column previously shown so you can get a better idea of why this re-arrangement is superior.

	A more logical/chronological arrangement of those ideas.	
[The individual ideas listed in this column should not call for any horizontal lines between ideas. Nor should the statements and questions (in columns 2 and 3, respectively) be written alongside any of the ideas listed in this first column.]	1. Your company manufactures the ABC machine. 2. An important component in that machine is made of aluminum castings. 3. Your machine requires the following specs for the castings used: a · · · · · · · · · · · b · · · · · · · · · · · c · · · · · · · · · · · ← d · · · · · · · · · · · e · · · · · · · · · · 4. You sometimes make your own castings and sometimes buy them from outside suppliers. 5. Your decision on whether to make or buy depends on the following factors: a. Economy of cost to make vs. cost to buy. b. Ready availability of needed supply. c. Adherence to specs. d. Maximum / optimum utilization of your own plant's overall facilities. 6. You have not yet bought any aluminum castings from us. 7. We make and sell the same kinds of castings to the other leading O.E.M.'s. 8. They are consistently and	Cy filled these in.

	A more logical/chronological arrangement of those ideas.	
	thoroughly pleased with our product and service.	
	9. We have ample facilities to accommodate you.	
	10. We know and agree with your policy of asking for quotes.	
	11. We want to quote on a reasonable volume.	
	12. In order to do that, we need some more specific information.	
	13. Please tell me:	
	. . . .	
	14. Do you want me to use a specific form for the quote (supplied by you) or will our form be acceptable?	
	15. I'll have it in your hands by next Wednesday.	

PREPARING THE MAGIC MAKE-HAPPEN QUESTIONS

Now we're ready to talk about how to formulate the questions we plan to ask during the sales call. Before getting back to Cy, let me state the principles involved in this technique. Some of what I will now say is repetitive of things I've told you before, but I want to set the whole concept down in one place, so you can see it in its entirety.

1. You want to get ready, the evening before, to ask questions of your prospect, this being the best way of both:

   a. Finding out earlier (rather than later) that you're on the wrong track (if you are), so you can either get on a better track (before wasting too much time) or realize on time that you'd better not spend any more time with him, at least that day.——and

   b. If it turns out that you *are* on the right track, continuing to involve him and getting him to sell himself on the very offer you want to sell to him.

2. You've already listed the sequence of ideas you'd like to get across (in

order to achieve your planned goal), arranged in the best logical/chronological manner possible.

3. There is no set formula that I know of which will assure you that you can easily convert each of those ideas from a statement to a good question. There are, however, some very re-assuring guides (which I will soon give you) to help you conceive the best question for each statement. Besides, I know from experience, in training large numbers of salesmen in the use of the Magic Question Technique, that after a few examples you will soon catch on to the basic device. From there on in, you will always be able to formulate easily the exact questions you need.

4. When you have finished filling in, properly, the second column of your worksheet, here's how you can begin to think of and write in the best questions in the third column:

   a. Take one statement at a time from the second column.
   b. Experiment with a few different questions that you can create until you come up with the one that is most likely to produce the answer already written down in the second column; wherever possible, avoid the type of question whose answer is merely *yes* or *no*. Sometimes *one* question will suffice for two or more statements.
   c. When you are satisfied with one question for that second-column statement, write the question down in the third column, alongside of the statement in the second column. Sometimes one statement will require two or more questions.

Here's an example of how Cy did it that evening.

A more logical/chronological arrangement of those ideas.	Questions I would like to ask to help me elicit some of those ideas from him.
1. Your company manufactures the ABC machine.	1. About how many ABC machines do you produce in one year?
2. An important component in that machine is made of aluminum castings.	2. What part is played in that machine by aluminum castings?
3. Your machine requires the following specs for the castings used: a . . . . b	3a. What are the specs you require for the castings you use in that machine?

A more logical/chronological arrangement of those ideas.	Questions I would like to ask to help me elicit some of those ideas from him.
c . . . . d . . . . e	3b. You didn't say anything about ... (a./b./c./d./e.). What role do they (does it) play in your spec requirements?
4. You sometimes make your own castings, and other times buy them from outside suppliers.	4. About what proportion of your required castings come from your own shop as compared to outside suppliers?
5. Your decision on whether to make or buy depends on the following factors: (a./b./c./d.).	5a. What factors determine your decision on whether to make or buy?
	5b. You didn't say anything about ... (a./b./c./d.). What role does it (do they) play in your decision?
6. You have not yet bought any aluminum castings from us.	6. What do you know about the aluminum castings we make?
7. We make and sell the same kinds of castings to the other leading O.E.M.'s.	7. We make and sell the same kinds of castings for these leading O.E.M.'s. Which ones do you know?
8. They are consistently and thoroughly pleased with our product and service.	8. What have you heard or read about our customers' satisfaction with our product and service?

A more logical/chronological arrangement of those ideas.	Questions I would like to ask to help me elicit some of those ideas from him.
9. We have ample facilities to accommodate you.	9. About what volume of aluminum castings do you require for your annual ABC production?
10. We know and agree with your policy of asking for quotes.	10. Do you order direct from the suppliers you use or do you have a policy of requiring quotes?
11. We want to quote on a reasonable volume.	11. What is the normal volume on which you require a single quote?
12. In order to do that, we need some more specific information. 13. Please tell me:	12/13. Since we definitely want to put in an appropriate quote at the right time, will you please give me the following specific information: . . . .
14. Do you want me to use a specific form for the quote (supplied by you) or will our form be acceptable?	14. Shall I use our own quote form or do you want to give me the form you require now?
15. I'll have it in your hands by next Wednesday.	15. Is Wednesday of next week satisfactory or would you rather I bring the completed quote in on the day after that?

FINAL STEPS IN GETTING READY

When you have completed your form, you should:

- Review it for completeness and applicability, making whatever changes, deletions or additions you think advisable.
- Study it in order to become well-acquainted with what it contains. I don't recommend memorizing it because:
    - —You may not need all of it.
    - —This would take too much time.
    - —You might sound like you're delivering a canned speech.
- Take it along with you on the itinerary which includes that call.

The Next Day

When you're getting ready to call on each prospect, try to find a few minutes to review the form so you'll be better able to remember its contents when you go in.

In a later chapter, I'll tell you how to make the best use of the make-happen planning you've done for this call.

ANOTHER CASE

Now let's take another situation and draw up a plan for the effective use of the magic formula of questions on the projected sales call.

I've selected an experience I had working with Percy Udall, an underwriter for the _____ Insurance Company.

Percy sold a variety of kinds of insurance to business executives. He planned on going to see the Chief Executive Officer of a medium-sized food processing company. The prospect had been suggested to him by an existing client of Percy's company, whom Percy had insured in a number of respects for many years, to the policy-holder's complete satisfaction.

As you probably know from your own experience, when A recommends B to you as a likely prospect, he doesn't always have too much information of a specific nature regarding the probability of a sale. Still, you must seek and accept such leads and pursue them in proportion to your other time requirements.

That's what happened to Percy. The recommendation included

only these bare statements:

- The prospect was the Chief Executive Officer of that company.
- He knew and valued the recommender.
- He was very intelligent, capable and progressive in his thinking.
- He was very receptive to new ideas and willing to listen to them.
- He was not "completely" covered with all the kinds of insurance he really needed.

Percy was able to get a certain amount of additional information (about the prospect and his company), but not enough to represent the kind of picture he liked to have before he went calling. So, he decided that his objective for the first (and maybe only) visit to that prospect was to probe and further qualify him as a prospect worth Percy's time and effort—either during the same visit or on one or more later interviews.

PERCY'S PLANNING

He and I worked together the evening before the day of the visit. Here's how Percy began to fill out the form.

Worksheet for Getting Ready to Close Through Sales Questions

Date of planned call 5/28/19_____
Time From 2 p.m. until about 3:30 p.m.
Prospect: _____, Chief Executive Officer of the_____Company.
Address: _____
How to get there: Route 23 north to exit 7. Right turn at light
                      until reaching _____ Street
Whom to see: _____Chief Executive Officer.

Objective for the visit:	To become better acquainted with the prospect. To learn as much as possible about him, his company and his insurance needs and existing coverage. On the chance that he may be a good prospect, to plant the seed that he serves his own best interests in buying his business-related insurance from me and my company. To arrange for whatever follow-up is best suited to what develops during the interview.

The Second Stage of the Planning

Now Percy was ready to fill in the columns on the form. Here are the statements that first occurred to him that evening, and the sequence in which he wrote them down in the first column (headed: **My first thinking on what message I'd like to get across to him during the call.**):

1. You probably are the most important single man in your company, and you therefore undoubtedly need key-man insurance.
2. Your present workmen's compensation setup may not be exactly what you need, and we have a very good plan for you.
3. A man like you probably hasn't done all the estate planning he should. We have an excellent approach to this need.
4. Every company of your size needs the right kind of group insurance: health, hospitalization, accident, life, etc. We have the best programs.
5. I can tailor exactly what you need, so here's the information I want to get from you.
6. I'll study all that information and get back to you with a definite program fitted exactly to what you need.
7. There's no charge for this study.

Columns two and three

Now Percy and I were ready to fill in the next two columns on the form. Here's how we worked out the second column.

A more logical/chronological arrangement of ideas.	Questions I would like to ask to help me elicit some of those ideas from him.
1. You are the Chief Executive Officer of your company.	
2. If your company has a certain kind and number of employees, you, the company and they need certain types of insurance.	
3. My company is the best in the business, and the coverage we offer people like you cannot be beaten.	
4. We are always interested in having clients like you, but our	

A more logical/chrono-logical arrangement of ideas.	Questions I would like to ask to help me elicit some of those ideas from him.
approach is strictly a tailored one.	
5. Therefore, neither you nor I can know how we may best serve you until I get certain information from you.	
6. I assure you that it will be worth your while to answer my questions.	
7. Here's the information I need from you:	
a. Your age and date of birth.	
b. A copy of your organization chart and position/job descriptions.	
c. The names, ages and dates of birth of your management people.	
d. Whether or not you have a union, and, if you do, a copy of the contract.	
e. What coverage you have, if any, for the following: (a./b./ etc.).	

A more logical/chronological arrangement of ideas.	Questions I would like to ask to help me elicit some of those ideas from him.
f. Your degree of satisfaction with your present coverage, with reasons.	
g. For you and each of your management people: ages, dates of birth and relationships of the members of immediate families.	
8. I shall take all this with me, have it studied by our experts and get back to you with a well-tailored plan.	
9. There will be no charge or obligation to you for this service.	
10. If it turns out that you really need some of our policies, I assure you that you will be getting the best possible setup from us.	
11. I'll phone you in about two weeks to set up our next appointment, at which time I'll be ready to present to you the best program that anyone can tailor for you.	

Planning the Questions

Next Percy and I turned our attention to getting ready for the actual interview, by converting column two into column three.

Here is what we came up with.

A more logical/chronological arrangement of ideas.	Questions I would like to ask to help me elicit some of those ideas from him.
1. You are the Chief Executive Officer of your company.	1. May I ask you, what is your official title in the company?
2. If your company has a certain kind and number of employees, you, the company and they need certain types of insurance.	2. a. About how many employees does your company have? b. How many are in top management? Middle management? c. What kinds of insurance does your company now have for the company, you and its employees? d. What kinds of insurance do you have for your first-line management and hourly paid employees?
3. My company is the best in the business, and the coverage we offer people like you cannot be beaten.	3. To what extent, if any, am I right in saying that you want the best possible coverage for your company and your people?
4. We are always interested in having clients like you, but our approach is strictly a tailored one.	4. To what extent is your present coverage tailored *exactly* to your needs?

A more logical/chrono-logical arrangement of ideas.	Questions I would like to ask to help me elicit some of those ideas from him.
5. Therefore, neither you nor I can know how we may best serve you until I get certain information from you.	5. From whom can I get the exact and accurate information I need in order to tailor your coverage to *your* exact needs?
6. I assure you that it will be worth your while to answer my questions.	6. When is the best time for you (him) to answer my questions so we can make the most valuable use of those questions I must ask?
7. Here's the information I need from you: a. Your age and date of birth.	7. a. How old are you and what is your birth-date?
b. A copy of your organization chart and position/job descriptions.	b. Please let me see (or let's draw up) your organization chart and position/job descriptions. (Not a question, but tantamount to one.)
c. The names, ages and dates of birth of your management people.	c. Please give me a list of your management people by name, with ages and dates of birth. (Or, let's draw it up.)
d. Whether or not you have a union, and, if you do, a copy of the contract.	d. What union(s), if any, do you have? When can I get a copy of the contract(s)?

A more logical/chronological arrangement of ideas.	Questions I would like to ask to help me elicit some of those ideas from him.
e. What coverage you have, if any, for the following: (a./b./ etc.).	e. For each of these men (women), what coverage do you now have (a./b./etc.)?
f. Your degree of satisfaction with your present coverage, with reasons.	f. For each of your present policies, to what extent are you not entirely satisfied, and why?
g. For you and each of your management people: ages, dates of birth and relationships of the members of immediate families.	g. For you and for each of these management people, what are the: ages, dates of birth and relationships in the respective, immediate families?
8. I shall take all this with me, have it studied by our experts and get back to you with a well-tailored plan.	8. I can have a well-tailored plan ready for you, based on expert judgment, within two weeks. Is June 15th better for you than the 16th?
9. There will be no charge or obligation to you for this service. 10. If it turns out that you really need some of our policies, I assure you that you will be getting the best possible setup from us.	9.-10. Since there will be no charge to you or obligation for this service, who else should I meet with today in order to make sure that the plan I present to you is exactly what you need? When is the best time to see him (them)?

A more logical/chrono-logical arrangement of ideas.	Questions I would like to ask to help me elicit some of those ideas from him.
11. I'll phone you in about two weeks to set up your next appoint-ment, at which time I'll be ready to present to you the best pro-gram that anyone can tailor for you.	11. I'd like to phone you in about two weeks to set up our next appointment and pre-sent this plan to you. What's the best day and time to phone you?

Summary

1. To the normal reasons for planning a sales call with *any* selling approach, add the special reasons for *effective* planning so essential to the successful use of the magic formula.
2. You *must* do your planning (for *any* technique) at a time when prospects are not available. This means either an evening or a weekend holiday.
3. The first step in any planning session is to review carefully all your records of previous contacts with the prospect.
4. Do as much qualifying of the prospect, in advance, as possible.
5. For *each* planned call, make sure you decide on the *exact* objective for that particular visit. Have alternative objectives available if you think this is wise.
6. Start your active planning by using the worksheet provided you, entitled: *Worksheet for Getting Ready to Close Through Sales Questions,* filling in the top and only the first column on the left.
7. Now take what you have put down in the first column and try to re-arrange your ideas in more logical and chronological sequence. Do this in the second column, numbering each idea in sequence and leaving plenty of space between ideas.
8. Next, go through each of those statements. For each of them:
     a. Try to think of a question which will elicit the response you have written down in the second column.
     b. When you come up with what you consider the best question, write it down in the third column, alongside the corresponding statement in the second column.
9. Learn the questions so you can ask them properly the next day—and really make things happen!

CHAPTER **3**

How to Use Your Sales Goals in Designing Persuasive Questions

In a previous chapter, I touched briefly on the importance of the right objectives in calling on prospects and making things happen. Now I'm going to develop that subject more fully.

First, let me re-state the essence of what I touched on before.

ULTIMATE OBJECTIVE OF ALL SELLING

In all kinds of companies, selling all kinds of products/services, the goal of the company for its salesmen, and the goal of the salesmen themselves, *must* be as follows:

- Constantly discover the maximum number of prospects available to that company.
- Continually qualify each prospect in order to determine:
    - Whether to concern oneself with him at all, for the present or the future.
    - If yes, when and how frequently.
    - The relative importance of each prospect to all the others, in order to establish priorities and visiting frequencies.
- As soon as possible, and at the right times, call on the best prospects (in descending order of advisability) with the most appropriate intermediate objectives.
- Do the best possible selling job on each call (with attendant telephone/letter follow-up, as appropriate) in order to:
    - Succeed in the intermediate objective.
    - Steadily advance the likelihood of achieving the ultimate objective.
    - Pave the way for the next contact.
- Wind up for each prospect with either:

—Firm and valid conclusions that there is no point in pursuing that particular prospect any more (or for a stated period of time before reviewing his status); or

—A successful sale (or series of continuing sales) to him under the following conditions:

1. He has bought absolutely everything from you that your company can provide him with, to his benefit.
2. He is thoroughly satisfied with everything he has bought from you.
3. You and your company are thoroughly satisfied with the relationship you have developed with that customer.
4. He has the best possible opinion of your company, its products/services, its integrity and reliability and its service to him.
5. You have established effective plans for continuing follow-up with him, including the successful sale to him of additional products/services that he can effectively use, whenever and as often as he can use them.
6. You have continually met your quotas (and, preferably, exceeded them maximally):
   a. Maximum/optimum coverage of prospects and customers for all valid objectives.
   b. Constant expansion of your prospecting and qualifying activities.
   c. Total sales volume.
   d. Product/service mix.
   e. Maximum/optimum profitability from your activities.

OBJECTIVE FOR ANY ONE CALL

Now, if you are confident that you can, on a planned visit, succeed in the ultimate objective of *all* selling, then by all means make that your intermediate (as well as ultimate) objective for the call, and plan the use of questions (during that call) in order to accomplish your objective. Bear this in mind, however:

- Whether the call you plan is the first visit to the prospect or not, you must be quite sure that you'll be able to *sell* him what you plan during that visit and come away with a *firm* commitment from him that he is buying or definitely will buy (within a stated period not too far off) exactly what you wanted to sell him.
- If you planned *that* objective and don't succeed in reaching it fully, you will

have *failed* in that call. You will have done less than your best. You will have wasted a certain amount of time trying to accomplish what you shouldn't have tried. You may have spoiled your chances (or, at least, hurt them) to accomplish a more realistic objective.

- Therefore, if there is a possibility that the *ultimate* objective may not be achievable on that call, you're better off planning an *intermediate* objective (leading, eventually, to that ultimate one) which you *can* succeed in reaching. Then, if it turns out, during the call that you *can* accomplish your ultimate objective, by all means move right into it.

- You may even want to plan two objectives for each visit: the probable intermediate one and the ultimate one.

My thesis, therefore, is: Plan for each visit an objective which is realistically achievable on that call, and which will ultimately lead to your final objective.

RELATIONSHIP BETWEEN OBJECTIVE AND CLOSE

Before moving into the matter of intermediate objectives, let's carefully define two important terms we shall be using all along.

1. *Objective:*   A goal for a sales contact. A reason why you want to communicate with the prospect. A result you want and hope to achieve through the contact.

2. *Close:*   The step(s) you take in order to achieve *that* objective. The prospect's firm commitment to you that he will do or say (or his actual doing or saying) what you want(ed) him to in pursuit of *that* objective.

In this connection, note the following:

You will be closing and achieving your objective for any one call if, at the end of that call, the prospect has either done or said what you wanted him to, or firmly committed himself (to that). Even if you walk away from that interview without a firm order, you have made things happen—*your way.*

If it is proper for you to set, as your objective for any one contact, the goal of coming away with a firm order, you haven't closed (and, therefore, you have failed to reach your objective) if you don't come away with it. If, however, you set an intermediate objective and succeed in it (without a firm order), you *have* closed and you *have* reached your valid objective.

Possible Intermediate Objectives

Now let's take up the different kinds of goals you may have for your calls, combining any two or more in one plan (as appropriate), or having one or more alternative goals for each call.

1. *Qualifying/prospecting.* This is the first time you are going to contact a prospect. Or you haven't contacted him for some time. Or circumstances have arisen which prompt you to bring yourself more up to date. Your goal here is to probe—either to decide he is a worthwhile prospect or get as much (additional) information about him as possible, which will help you establish and pursue additional valid objectives.

2. *Arranging to see the right person.* The only objective referred to here is to find out, and/or take steps to see, the right person(s) to contact for a valid, planned objective.

3. *Finding out the best objective.* If you are confident that you should interview a prospect, but aren't sure what your objective should be, you want to probe in order to decide what it should be.

4. *First introduction to the prospect.* You have never called on him (or it's been too long ago, or you want to talk about something new to him). You feel it's worthwhile to take the time to introduce yourself and tell him about your company and its product(s)/service(s), leading to his knowledge, understanding and/or appreciation.

5. *Take the first or next step.* In order to make an effective, overall presentation, you need two or more visits, each leading to the next. This particular call must establish in his mind certain elements of your presentation so that you can continue on the next call with the next essential element(s), which cannot effectively be completed during this planned call (first or later).

6. *Get approval to bid.* The prospect requires bids before he can or will award an order. He doesn't accept bids from everyone.

7. *Help write specs.* The prospect has (or will soon have) specs for what he will buy. You want those specs to coincide with what you have to offer. You want him to let you help him write those specs.

8. *Get specs for bids.*

He will accept a bid from you. He will have certain specs for that bid. You want to know what they are.

9. *Help determine consumption.*

Your prospect will offer for sale, to others, what you want to sell him. He will buy from you in proportion to the re-sale potential. He wants a survey made. You want permission to do this (or to present your previously surveyed data).

10. *Motivate dealers (distributors).*

You want to motivate them to promote/sell your products/services more effectively.

11. *Motivate use of promotions.*

You want him to use more of your or his advertising and promotional campaigns/materials.

12. *Work with dealer salesmen.*

You want permission to work with the dealers/distributors/salesmen or merchandisers in order to increase/improve the sale of your products/services.

13. *Arrange for visits/specialists.*

You want him to come to your company to see things/activities/people there, or you want permission to bring in specialists.

14. *Get permission for tests.*

You want him to test your product/service, or you want permission to test it yourself for his needs.

15. *Arrange for tailoring.*

You want to tailor a product or service to his specific needs. You want to arrange for this within the limits of cost acceptable to both of you.

16. *Get information on progress.*

You've put in a bid or arranged for a test. You want to know what's happening, how you stand and what, if anything else, you can and should do.

17. *Firm, final commitment.*

You are ready to get a firm commitment from the prospect to say or do something at once (or in the very near future) which represents an order (or, in cases like the detailmen who call on doctors, a definite assurance that he will say or do something leading to the purchase of your product/service).

18. *Follow-up.*

You want to find out his degree of satisfaction with what you sold or promised him, and/or whether/when he's ready for your next objective.

19. *Keeping in touch.*

You want him to know that you're always interested in him. You want to maintain rapport. You want to find out when he's ready for anything else you can do for him.

20. *Satisfying a complaint.*

You've gotten word that he's not entirely happy with the product/service or any other relationship with you or your company. You want to get all the facts and relevant opinions. You want to assure him that the matter will be resolved to his complete satisfaction.

21. *Prospecting.*   You want him to recommend others to you.

DESIGNING QUESTIONS FOR GOALS

The important message here is:

—Always know what your precise objective/objectives/alternative objective(s) are before you go any further in your planning. If you're not in a position to do this, then either:

  • Make your aim to establish an objective; or
  • Be ready to switch to a valid objective in the early moments of the interview.

—Plan your statements and questions around the objective(s) you have decided on.

Now let's take a number of cases from real life. Each situation is somewhat different from the others. For each one I'll give:

  • The prospect, type of product/service and objective.
  • The details of the second and third columns (in brief) of the planning worksheet I've already recommended.

Prospect; product; objective	Basic logic/chronology	Questions
1. Heavy-Equipment Distributor; tractors; take a next step: get him to want to carry a second tractor line.	a. You presently represent the XYZ company and sell its tractors to your customers.	a. What tractors do you now carry?
	b. You don't carry any other tractor line.	b. What other tractor line do you carry?
	c. The distributor who carries at least two lines has the following advantages over the one who carries at least two lines:	c. In carrying only the one line, how do you arrange for the following essential services to your prospective and actual customers?

Prospect; product; objective	Basic logic/chronology	Questions
	(1) He can sell his tractors to people who are already firmly convinced they want the (an) other line.	(1) Providing them with a tractor they want when they definitely don't want the one you have.
	(2) He can broaden the chances of selling a tractor at all, by having more than one line.	(2) Having an alternative line as an additional sales tool.
	(3) He can seek and satisfy a different, additional market.	(3) Reaching a different, additional market.
	(4) He can sell more parts (for two lines) than where he carries only one line.	(4) Increasing the profit from selling parts.
	(5) He can service more tractors.	(5) Increasing the profit from servicing more than one kind of tractor.
	(6) He can attract more customers for other products.	(6) Attracting more customers for other products.
	d. If anything happened to your ability to deliver your present line, you'd have an alternative line.	d. Selling at least some tractors if you couldn't get enough of the right kind of your present line when you needed them.
	e. If your present line isn't as complete as a second line, you can	e. Ability to sell more customers where your present line

Prospect; product; objective	Basic logic/chronology	Questions
	cover more customers.	may not be as complete as they'd like it to be.
	f. You ought to look into a good second line like mine.	f. What second line do you now know enough about in order to be able to make the right decision?
2. Packaging Engineer of O.E.M.; air cap; get permission to run a demonstration.	a. You package your product in a certain way.	a. How do you now package your product?
	b. It's extremely important that the air not escape from your package.	b. How important to you is the sealing of your package to prevent the escape of air?
	c. The device you require for preventing that escape must meet the following requirements (a., b., c., etc.)	c. What requirements do you set for any device you use to prevent the escape of air?
	d. You didn't mention the following requirements:	d. Why didn't you mention the following requirements...?
	e. Your present air-escape prevention device is not doing for you what is best for your packaging, for the following reasons:	e. What effect does it have on your profitable packaging that your present device lacks...?
	f. You certainly should	f. How do you intend

Prospect; product; objective	Basic logic/chronology	Questions
	look into another device that is superior for your needs—mine.	to find a better device, more suited to your needs?
	g. What you should do is let me run a demonstration for you on how my device meets *all* of your needs, better than all others on the market.	g. Who besides yourself (if anyone) should witness a demonstration of my device?
	h. I want to set up a time and place for this, now.	h. In the next week, what day and time shall I be here, and where in your plant?
3. Tool Distributor; industrial handgun; get him to handle the line.	a. You have a large number of industrial customers who use industrial handguns.	a. How many of your present industrial customers use industrial handguns?
	b. They are buying those tools elsewhere because you don't carry them.	b. Where are they buying them and why?
	c. You are probably losing many actual and potential customers for your present lines because you don't carry our line.	c. How many of your present and potential customers are you losing because they can buy everything they need in one place?
	d. Our line is very profitable to you, as follows:	d. What do you think would be the profit to you if you handled our line?

Prospect; product; objective	Basic logic/chronology	Questions
	e. Our line is exactly what is wanted by your prospects and customers, as follows:	e. What do your customers want in an industrial handgun?
	f. With our line you have an exclusive in your area, under very favorable terms, as follows:	f. How important to you would these terms be: . . . . . .
	g. We must have a reliable distributor in your area right away and would prefer it to be you.	g. When may I come back to discuss this contract, which I'll leave with you (before I go to see another distributor in the area who is interested)?
4. TV Station Chief Engineer; radiating antennas; help him write specs.	a. You are presently engaged in looking for an antenna system different from the one you are now using.	a. How much longer will you be using the antenna system you now have?
	b. Before you decide to consider any new antenna system, you will ask potential suppliers to submit bids on specs you will supply them.	b. How will you go about deciding where to look and what to consider among all the possible suppliers?
	c. You haven't written your specs yet.	c. What specs do you now have?
	d. You are going to call	d. What criteria will

Prospect; product; objective	Basic logic/chronology	Questions
	on the best people you can find to help you write those specs.	you employ in selecting those who are to help you write those specs?
	e. You haven't yet found anyone, either within your organization or outside of it, who meets *all* of those criteria.	e. Have you found anyone who meets all of those criteria?
	f. We are the most qualified people anywhere to help you write those specs.	f. Let's take each criterion for writing specs, one at a time. For each one, let's see who meets it to your complete satisfaction. Who meets them all as well as we do?
	g. We want to send our Mr. Jones to meet with you, to write those specs, just as soon as possible.	g. Will you be ready to work with our spec-writing expert next Tuesday?
5. President of manufacturing company; tailored mailing brochure; firm commitment.	a. You rely on mailings for the profitable promotion of your manufactured products.	a. How do you promote your manufactured products?
	b. Once each half-year you put out a new or revised brochure for mailing.	b. How frequently do you revise or update your mailing brochure?

Prospect; product; objective	Basic logic/chronology	Questions
	c. Your brochures require the following characteristics: (1) Size: . . . . (2) Number of folds: . . (3) Colors: . . . . (4) Copy: . . . . (5) Photos/drawings: . . (6) Layout/design: . . . (7) Paper quality: . . . (8) Type size: . . . . . (9) Mailer facility: . . .	c. What are the requirements for your brochures? . . . What are they for: (1), (2), etc.?
	d. You require . . . lead time between the beginning of the decision to prepare the brochure and the date of mailing.	d. From the moment you decide to re-do your brochure, until you want it mailed out, what is the general lead time?
	e. You don't use an advertising agency.	e. Who writes your copy for you? Does your layout? Does your graphics?
	f. You want unlimited consultation, guidance and help.	f. How often do you require consultation with your supplier?
	g. You want your supplier to take care of the whole processing and mailing procedure for you.	g. Who will do the processing and mailing for you?
	h. You will want . . . number of copies.	h. How many copies will you want printed?

Prospect; product; objective	Basic logic/chronology	Questions
	i. You will want to place your order in two weeks.	i. How soon can you be ready to place your order if you are to be finished by . . .?
	j. You'll have to know now how much this is going to cost you.	j. With whom shall I sit down now to draw up a firm, accurate cost to you for each detail of the complete job?.
	k. I'll want to get right back to you today after he and I finish that.	k. Where will you be today to sign the order?
6. Marketing Manager; hotel convention facilities; prospecting/qualifying.	a. Your good friend, . . ., has told me that you plan to hold a sales meeting in the spring of next year.	a. When do you plan to hold your next sales meeting?
	b. You will require a hotel with certain specific facilities, like:	b. What facilities do you require for your sales meetings? How about these facilities: . . . .
	c. We are equipped to handle effectively a specific range of numbers of people.	c. About how many people will participate in your meeting?
	d. We gear our service and price to the schedule.	d. What is your planned schedule: days, times, activities, accommodations needed?

Prospect; product; objective	Basic logic/chronology	Questions
	e. You will want to see our setup, at no cost to you.	e. Can you come and see us some time this week, or do you want to send your representative?
7. Purchasing Agent of processing plant; new chemical; arrange to see right person.	a. You use the XYZ type of chemical in your process.	a. In which of your various processes do you use the XYZ chemical?
	b. Our XYZ chemical is new, most effective and probably very important to you.	b. When may I tell you about our new XYZ chemical, which I am confident will make that process much more effective?
	c. Since you say that you are not in a position to evaluate it yourself, I'd like to see the man who is.	c. When can I see him? Is he available now, or would tomorrow morning be better?
	d. I want to make the arrangements necessary to see him, and, also, to get back to you.	d. Can you get him on the phone now, or should I call him? And, when can I report back to you?
8. Purchasing Agent for large complex of offices; office services; find out best objective.	a. You have a large complex of offices requiring many services, like: (1) Evening cleaning. (2) Window washing. (3) Towels. (4) Furniture polishing. (5) Water cooler. (6) Coffee makers.	a. What kinds of services do your offices require? . . . How come you didn't mention: (1), (2), etc?

Prospect; product; objective	Basic logic/chronology	Questions
	b. We offer a large variety of services for offices like yours and are eager to offer you only what you need.	b. Which of those services are you not getting, either at all or to your complete satisfaction?
9. Building Contractor; lumber; first introduction.	a. We've never met before because both of us have been too busy, but we ought to find out how the two of us can benefit from a mutual business relationship.	a.(1) About how much lumber do you consume a month? (2) How much do you know about my company and its products and services?
	b. Our company has been serving the following contractors in this area for 15 years:	b. Here is a list of the contractors we've been serving satisfactorily for the last 15 years. Which ones do you know?
	c. Our lumber supply is of top grade, great variety and competitively priced.	c. Who besides yourself in the company should have a copy of this catalogue?
	d. Our facilities and reliability for service are well-known in this area.	d. Please read these few testimonials from selected customers .... Which of these men would you like to contact for further details?
	e. You ought to see our yard.	e. When would it be most convenient for you to come and visit us—this week or next?

Prospect; product; objective	Basic logic/chronology	Question
	f. I've been assigned to work with you and will contact you periodically, in order to be able to serve you with what you need exactly when you need it.	f. When are the best times for me to come and see you?
10. Controller; E.D.P. programming; third call.	a. I know you aren't ready, yet, to subscribe to our payroll service, but I want to make sure I'm giving you all the help I can.	a. Now that you've studied our proposal, what questions do you have?
	b. Now that I've answered all the questions you had, I'd like you to sign this order.	b. When do you want to start the service—this week or next?
	c. Since I cannot really disagree with the validity of your reason for not being ready to sign today, I want to try to make my next visit lead to an order.	c. What still remains to be done before you are ready to give me a firm order?
	d. I'd like to come back next week to firm up the order.	d. Which day is best for you next week: Wednesday or Thursday?
11. U.S. Government Department Purchasing Agent; industrial fasteners;	a. Your Department uses industrial fasteners.	a. What kinds of industrial fasteners does your Department use?
	b. You consider sup-	b. How can my com-

Prospect; product; objective	Basic logic/chronology	Questions
get approval to bid.	pliers only by bid.	pany become a supplier for your Department?
	c. I want to get on your bid list.	c. What do we have to do to get on your Department's bid list?
	d. I'd like the forms at once.	d. If I get the forms from you now, when is the earliest I can submit our first bid?
12. Manager, large industrial building; smoking urns for elevator lobbies; follow-up.	a. Last month you bought 100 of our smoking urns.	a. When did you receive the smoking urns you ordered from me last month?
	b. I want to be sure that the order was delivered exactly as desired.	b. How many were delivered? . . . On what day and time? . . . How did the delivery fit in with your receiving schedule? . . . Were any of them dented, or were they all perfect?
	c. I want to make sure that you are entirely satisfied with the way in which they solved your problems regarding smokers waiting for elevators or getting off them.	c. What have you heard from your tenants about the convenience of the urns? . . . Their attractiveness? . . . The ease of emptying them and keeping them clean? . . . Their durability? . . . Your tenants' satisfaction with them?

Prospect; product; objective	Basic logic/chronology	Questions
	d. I'd like to come away, today, with a good order.	d. When may I send you 25 more urns for your other building? . . . How many plants do you have in your buildings which require sturdy and attractive metal containers?
13. Agricultural Products Dealer; sales promotion materials; get him to use them.	a. You carry our line of feed; the more you sell of it the greater the profit to you. We have statistics to show the demand in your area for our feed.	a. How much have you got in stock now of our feed? . . . When was the last time you made a study of the demand for it.
	b. By not turning our feed over as frequently as the demand requires, you're diminishing your profits from feed sales and losing customers.	b. How much potential profit have you lost from not selling all of the feed demanded? . . . About how many of your customers have you lost as a result?
	c. You must get all the customers who want our feed to come back to you and buy not only the feed but many of the other products you carry, which they are now getting elsewhere.	c. How do you plan to get all your former and potential customers back, to buy our feed and all the other products you carry that they're now buying elsewhere?
	d. You'll want to do this effectively, inexpensively and at once.	d. About how much do you think this should cost you?

Prospect; product; objective	Basic logic/chronology	Questions
	e. I'd like you to see this sales promotion item we've devised for you, how it works, how to display it, why you should take it on at once and how inexpensive it is.	e. (1) Where do you think this display would attract the attention of most farmers who pass by?
		(2) What questions do you have on how it works?
		(3) If it brings in ten new customers a week, how much additional profit do you think it will bring you?
		(4) Since the display is free with a $100 order, when would you like this effective promotion piece?
14. Office Manager; desks; satisfy a complaint.	a. My company has referred your communication to me, about the desks we recently sent you.	a. When did you receive the desks you wrote us about?
	b. I understand you indicated that the desk drawers don't open easily enough.	b. How many of the desks are causing you some concern?
	c. I want to make sure of the exact nature of the problem.	c. Exactly what is the difficulty?
	d. I'd like to see this for myself.	d. When may I have a look?

Prospect; product; objective	Basic logic/chronology	Questions
	e. Both my company and I are extremely sorry about this. There are extenuating circumstances, but the important thing is to get the matter straightened out at once, to your complete satisfaction—and that we shall do!	e.(1) Besides apologizing to *you* for the inconvenience, is there anyone else to whom we can explain how unavoidable this was? (2) How soon may I send our repairman to make the few adjustments necessary to put the drawers into completely satisfactory condition?
	f. I want to be sure, now, that I've taken care of your *complete* complaint.	f. What else can I do now to put things entirely right?
15. Owner-Contractor of Supply Warehouse; paint; get approval to go out with his salesmen.	a. You carry my line of paints, but I'm not satisfied that they're moving fast enough for your profit (and service to your customers in other lines) and my company's ability to continue to have you represent our line.	a.(1) Why doesn't our paint move as fast here as it does in the other warehouses which carry our line? (2) What do you think of these profit figures for those other warehouses which carry our paint?
	b. I have good reason to believe that your salesmen in the field aren't promoting our paints as effectively as they should.	b. What figures do you have on the saturation by your field salesmen of the enormously profitable market for our paints? ... How do their results compare

Prospect; product; objective	Basic logic/chronology	Questions
		to these figures, which we've compiled?
	c. You don't have the time to train and motivate your men to increase your profits by such saturation.	c.(1) Why aren't your men coming anywhere near to saturating that potential?
		(2) How important is our line to you?
		(3) How much time will you be able to spend with your men in the next two months to train and motivate them enough to reach the goals we set for them?
	d. I'm eager to take this on for you at no cost to you.	d. Since I'm ready to help you with this, and feel it should be started right away, do you prefer that I set up the schedule with you, or individually with each man? . . . Can we begin tomorrow, or would Thursday be better for you?
16. Personnel Manager; catering service; prospecting.	a. You have indicated to me that you are enthusiastic about the catering service we are now running for you.	a. What's your most up-to-date evaluation of the catering service we're running for you?

Prospect; product; objective	Basic logic/chronology	Questions
	b. You certainly should want to make it possible for your business associates to benefit in the same way.	b. What do you think would be the reaction to your helpfulness if you made it possible for other businessmen you know to benefit in the same way.
	c. You'd be helping them, yourself and me if you referred me to them?	c. Which of them would be grateful to you for telling them about us?
	d. I'd like you to refer me to as many prospects as possible who can most benefit from our service, and give me as much information about them as will help me.	d. Who are the most likely prospects, and what can you tell me about them which will help me serve them best?
	e. I'd like to use you as a reference.	e. To which of them may I say you referred me?
17. Oil Well Developer; pipe; get latest information on progress of bid.	a. We submitted our bid a month ago, and we know that the final decision won't be made until the middle of this month.	a. Is the bid deadline still what it was a month ago, or has there been a change?
	b. While we submitted our best bid, things may have changed with either you, our competitors or us, and, if that's so, we	b. What changes, if any, have there been in the bid situation?

Prospect; product; objective	Basic logic/chronology	Questions
	want to be sure we're still making you our best offer.	
	c. We're in a position now to make certain adjustments, if we can still make our desired profit with a better offer.	c. How can we make sure that changed circumstances can be met by us with a reconsideration better for each of us?
	d. We'd like to know where we stand on our bid and what, if anything, we can do to make sure we win it.	d. What can you legitimately tell me which will guide me in assuring myself that we're still making you the best offer we can?
18. Large industrial company; office layout and equipment; get permission to bring in specialist.	a. You have indicated that you want all of your offices redesigned and redecorated.	a. How many of your offices are you ready to have re-designed right away?
	b. You are satisfied that we can do exactly the kind of job for you that you want.	b. What additional criteria do you want to tell me about in order to round out your complete satisfaction with our ability to do the job exactly as you want it?
	c. The next step has to be a careful, detailed analysis by our expert layout man.	c. With whom should our layout expert work?

Prospect; product; objective	Basic logic/chronology	Questions
	d. Both you and he need to make an appointment in advance, and real soon.	d. Whom should our Mr. Jones phone for an appointment, and when this week is best for him to phone?
19. Large Super-Market Manager; waste removal; just keep in touch.	a. Our pickup service at your back door is going along real fine.	a. What are we not doing for you that we should be?
	b. I know you are presently buying from us all the service you need, and we're very pleased with that.	b. When can our President phone you, to express his appreciation of all the fine business you're giving us?
	c. I just wanted to visit with you to tell you that we're always ready to help you whenever you need us.	c. How much time can you spare me now for a simple visit of appreciation? . . . What can I do for you now to make our very satisfactory relationship even more so?
	d. If I don't get a chance to come to see you soon, please phone me if there's anything else you need.	d. When do you think it would be wise for me to touch base with you again?

Summary

1. While the *ultimate* goal of every sales call is to contribute to a firm order or commitment, you can't always expect to get one on a first call on a particular prospect, or, in many cases, on a second or third call.
2. Whenever it is realistic to strive for a firm commitment on *each* sales call, by all means make that your goal; but if any one call isn't likely to make things happen:
     a. Select for that call an objective which *is* realistic (and appropriate).
     b. Bear in mind, during *every* call that your *ultimate* goal (the sooner the better) is to get an order.
     c. Make the objective of each call on one prospect lead, as soon as possible, to the achievement of the ultimate goal.
3. For each call you plan set an objective, but be armed with alternative objectives in the event that the one you anticipated doesn't turn out to be the best one.
4. Plan your questions to elicit from the prospect the statements which will lead to the goal you've set; if you can't get those replies, switch objectives or decide whether or not it might be better to come back some other time.

CHAPTER 4

How to Use Make-Happen Questions for Keeping the Customer Interested

ATTENTION

You should say nothing unless you are absolutely sure that the buyer:

—Is listening to or watching *only* what you are saying or doing.

—Is making every effort to hear/see and understand *only* what *you* are at that time saying or doing.

This is what is meant by his paying *attention* to you at all times during the interview.

Before I discuss how to *attract* his attention through magic make-happen questions, I want to review with you the importance of, and techniques for, *keeping* his attention throughout the interview. This divides itself into two separate but concurrent types of activities:

1. You must always be so interesting in what you say and do that he *wants* to give his undivided attention to only you. Here the question approach can't be beaten, as we shall soon see.

2. You must *stop* talking or doing the very moment that a potential interruption comes to your notice, wait until the interruption is all ended and pick up again, far enough back to bring his train of thought to where it was before the interruption. During the interruption you should maintain a neutral stance, and when you resume, do so without any display of annoyance. Introduce your resumption with your last statement/question or two, preceded by something like: "We had agreed that. . . ." or, "You were saying that. . . ." or, "I was asking you. . . ."

The most frequent kinds of interruptions you must be on the lookout for are:

• Someone has just begun to come into the room where you two are. Wait until the individual is out of the room.

- The phone has just begun to ring. Wait until he has finished both the conversation and the notes he may want to make right away.
- He has to go out for a while. Wait until he is seated and seems ready for you.
- He begins to do something which you know is unrelated to your objective.

INTEREST

A relationship important to the effective use of questions is the degree of *interest* the prospect takes in what the salesman says. To make things happen through interest, you must couch everything you say and do in terms of what it will do for *him*. This is another way of saying that you must talk *benefits* to him, not *features* of your product or service; although, you may have to back up the statement of a benefit with supporting features.

I'll present examples of this, and show how to use questions effectively for that purpose, later on. Now let's come back to *attention*.

CAPTURING ATTENTION

Before I go into the technique for using attention-getting questions, let's talk about *capturing* the attention of your prospect at the outset of the interview. I want, first, to analyze with you the situation you find yourself in when you first come into the presence of the prospect.

Before you come in, he either:

—Is still thinking about something which occurred before that; or
—Has just begun to think of something unrelated to you; or
—He isn't thinking about anything.

And any or all of this can be true even if he's expecting your visit.

Your Job

Since this is the case, what must you do?

First of all, you must not begin to try to advance your basic offer until you have his undivided attention. This means that you must capture his attention, as soon as possible after you come in, *away* from where it was, to where you want it to be.

This leads to the whole question of the opening moments of a sales call.

INTRODUCTION

Many salesmen believe that they should always begin their interview with what can be called *small talk*. I don't want to take up your time telling you why they want to do this. I do, however, want to tell you why they *shouldn't* do this in the particular way they do.

In order to make this clear, I have to tell you how I use the term.

Small talk is conversation, initiated—usually—by the salesman (or pursued by him when the prospect starts it), which has no direct bearing on (and doesn't lead directly to) the proposition you'd like to close during that call.

Extent of Allowability

Let me first tell you about the few cases where I feel small talk is permissible, or, at least, unavoidable.

—If the prospect initiates it, you try to put a polite but firm end to it so you can quickly get on with your goal.

—If this is a second or subsequent call on a prospect, and you know of something which he is dying to talk about (like the fact that his daughter is graduating from college, or that his wife was ill and she's getting better), you politely mention it—briefly—and try to prevent him from dwelling on it too long.

Why No Small Talk

Aside from the limited cases listed just above, you should not initiate (and should discourage his initiation of) small talk, for the following reasons:

• It takes precious minutes away from the time available to you for your important communications.

• It distracts from your main emphases.

• It may be motivated by your unconscious desire to postpone the moment when he will say *no*.

• Its ostensible purpose (to soften him up, etc.) is much more effectively (and less wastefully) achieved by establishing and maintaining with him the right kind of rapport (which I shall soon discuss).

RECOMMENDED OPENERS

You can use questions for openers in sales calls to make things happen. The questions used should apply to two different situations: a first call on a prospect and all subsequent calls.

First call

If this is the first time you are to meet the prospect, I suggest the following sequence of openers:

1. Immediately begin to establish rapport (to be discussed below), which should be nurtured and maintained throughout the relationship.
2. Nod to him, put your card on his desk and tell him how pleased you are he is seeing you.
3. Wait until you are seated.
4. Immediately capture his attention (devices below), and remember always to talk in terms of *his* interest.
5. Tell him you're there only to be of service to *him,* and that you can best do this by finding out the extent to which what you have to offer really can benefit him.
6. That's why you must ask him some questions.
7. Start right in with your questions.

Subsequent calls

1. Nod to him and thank him for seeing you this time.
2. Wait until you're seated.
3. Immediately capture his attention and assure his interest.
4. Tell him that, as usual, you want to make sure you will be of continuing service to him.
5. That's why you must again ask him some questions.
6. Start right in with your questions.

Rapport

When you go in to see a prospect, the first thing he becomes aware of is you. Before you get a chance to try to convince him that he should commit himself to what you want, he is already evaluating *you.* Here's what he is asking himself, consciously or otherwise:

- Do I like what I see in this man?
- Do I feel comfortable with him?
- Does he seem to stand for the same things that I do?
- Am I being distracted, by things *about* him, from what he wants to say and do?
- Does he seem to be interested in *me?*
- Is he interesting to listen to and watch?

Now, if he forms and maintains a favorable impression of you, along those lines, he will:

—Give you his undivided attention.
—Want to go along with you as much as he can.

—Be receptive to any reasonable proposition you may have for him.
—Be more likely to let you convince him of your offer.

But the opposite is also true. If he doesn't have a favorable impression of you, he will:

a. Stop paying attention.
b. Be unreceptive to your ideas.
c. Want to get rid of you as soon as possible.

This means that from the very first moment you become acquainted with him, until the moment you leave him for the last·time—in all of your contacts with him—you must maintain the relationship I've described.

What's more, if you want to ask him questions, rapport becomes more important than ever, because:

1. If he feels properly toward you, he will be most delighted to have you ask him questions.
2. With rapport between you, he'll want to answer you fully and honestly.

Attention, Again

Now let's get back to the subject of attention.

Once you have his attention, and have allowed properly for interruptions, the question arises: How do you keep his attention all through the interview? Here are the most important ways:

1. You must really believe—and constantly convey by your attitude and its manifestations—that the combination of your product/service, your company and yourself cannot be beaten by anyone, and is exactly what he needs.
2. You must continue to maintain rapport.
3. Most important of all: Ask the right questions all along and listen attentively to his answers, guiding your next statements or questions by his reactions to *your* questions.

Interest, Again

How can you translate the statements *you want to make* into statements *he wants to hear?* The many different kinds of examples I shall give you are from my own joint calls and joint-call planning, with salesmen I've gone out on the road with, as well as from my own selling activities.

Statements I want to make to my prospect.	Questions I can ask which make *him* interested in what I want to say
My system is time saving.	How much time do you think this new system will save you?
My price is competitive.	How much is your present equipment costing you to maintain each month? How much of a saving would please you?
I need to know the specs you require for the job.	What specs do you quite properly insist on for the satisfactory performance of a supplier?
Our technical experts are the best in the trade.	What kind of technical assistance would you welcome?
By buying from us, you get the best service anywhere.	How does your immediate superior react to your ability to get the best service available anywhere?
My spaghetti packages are more salable than their competition.	What is the percentage of demand for the different brands of spaghetti available for stores like yours?
Our advertising program is more effective than any of our competitors'.	How much direct help are you now getting from your present suppliers' consumer advertising programs?
Our packaging is much more attractive than that of the competition.	What statistics do you have on the reactions of your customers to the packaging you now offer them?
There is no waste when you use my chemicals.	What percentage of waste do you presently have with the chemicals you are now using?

Statements I want to make to my prospect.	Questions I can ask which make *him* interested in what I want to say
My containers can be stored with a minimum of space.	How much space does one of your present containers occupy?
My paint is easier to apply to your assembly.	What problems do you have with the application of the paint you are now using?
My company's gas is safer to handle than any other gas.	What is your safety record with the handling of the gas you are now using?
My yarn will sell more profitably than the ones you are now carrying.	What is the history of profitability of sale of the yarns you are now carrying?
By carrying my complete line, you will be able to meet *all* of your customers' demands.	What percentage of your actual and potential customers are disappointed because you don't carry one particular item that they want?
My company offers you better field service than the competition.	What kind of field service is your present supplier giving you?
Our warehouses are closer to your plants than any other suppliers'.	How close are your present suppliers' warehouses to your various plants?
We work more closely with your salesmen than any other company.	How frequently do your present suppliers go out in the field with your salesmen?
Our cold cups hold the contents at the desired temperature for a longer period than the competitive cups.	How long do your present cups keep the contents cold?
Our gears last longer than any others.	With what frequency do you have to change your present gears?
You get a better deal if you buy from me in larger quantity.	What quantity can you effectively dispose of in one year?

Statements I want to make to my prospect.	Questions I can ask which make *him* interested in what I want to say
Our forklifts require less maintenance than the competitors' equipment.	How frequently do you have to take a forklift out of use for repairs?
The most successful banks in this state are using our computer time.	What information do you have on the more successful banks in this state?
By using our machine, you have to stock fewer spare parts.	How many different kinds of spare parts do you now have to stock for your present machine?
We offer a life-time guarantee with our installation.	How much is it now costing you to keep your present installation in constant efficiency?
We can send a man to your plant within two hours of your reporting a breakdown.	What do you consider a good time lapse between a breakdown and the arrival of a serviceman?
Our inventory control system is the best you can have.	What do you require in an inventory control system? What aspects of your present system fail to meet those requirements?
With our frozen foods, you can get the best markup possible.	What is your present markup on the frozen foods you are now offering to your customers?
The availability of our administrative services is limited and will soon be difficult to obtain.	How long can you afford to wait to have those records and reports completed for the government agencies calling for them?
By offering our farm equipment, you will get a better return on your investment.	What return are you now getting on your investment in the farm equipment you are now stocking?
With our layout and design service, you'll be able to maximize and optimize the space you now	How many office employees do you need in this area? What is the average square footage per

Statements I want to make to my prospect.	Questions I can ask which make *him* interested in what I want to say
have available for your office needs.	employee? What surveys have you made on the degree of efficiency they yield with the space they have?
Our dresses do not shrink if properly washed.	What do your customers say about dress shrinkage from washing?
Our potato chips meet the most stringent government standards.	When was the last time a government food inspector came to visit your store? What did he say about these potato chips you are now featuring?
Your customers will more readily buy our product because it is a well-known brand name.	What statistics do you have on customer preference for soaps by brand name?
Our company is completely reliable.	What kind of dependability do you look for in a supplier?
My company can advise you on financing your purchase of this investment apartment house, to your complete satisfaction.	What financing problems do you see if you buy this apartment house for investment purposes?
Our denture frames lend themselves more easily to the work you have to do for the dentists employing your services.	What role does the denture frame play in your ability to give the dentist the kind of service he wants?
You're better off buying direct from us than through a wholesaler.	What advantages do you have from buying these drug items from the wholesaler? How do they compare with these advantages of buying direct from us?
My company will give you full credit for all returns.	What is your present arrangement on credit for items you can't sell within a month?

Statements I want to make to my prospect.	Questions I can ask which make *him* interested in what I want to say
Our displays will not only help sell particular products but will also add to the general attractiveness of your store.	What do you look for in a display? How does it help sell a particular product? What effect does it have on the customer's general attraction to your store?
Our laboratory has the best technicians in your area.	What degree of technical proficiency do you require in your laboratory needs?
We provide the most frequent pickup and delivery service in this business.	What's the schedule of pickup and delivery your present cleaners and launderers are now offering you?
More and more people are buying power tools because they are now doing by themselves what they used to have done for them by commercial outfits.	What is the percentage of increase in the last year of people doing by themselves what they used to have done for them by mechanics or carpenters? How many of the people represented by this increase are buying their own power tools?
You are better off leasing your trucks from us than owning your own.	What are the elements of cost to you in owning, operating and maintaining your own trucks? How do these elements compare to the cost and service available to you by leasing from us, as, for example: . . . . ?
Our equipment will cut down materially on your handling costs.	What does it now cost you to handle your materials from the beginning of the assembly line to the end of the line?
Our heating systems will be a positive inducement to your prospective tenants.	What do your prospective tenants want in a heating system? How do you propose to give them this to convince them that

Statements I want to make to my prospect.	Questions I can ask which make *him* interested in what I want to say
	your system is a strong reason for taking the apartment?
Discerning restaurant patrons return to those restaurants whose food is consistently tasty.	What experience have you had with patron reaction to the quality of beef that you provide them with? How many indications have you had that they feel their steaks are not always of the same quality?
Our printing establishment is open around the clock and around the year, always staffed with an adequate supply of workers.	How often do you need work done in a hurry? How many print shops do you know that can give you overnight service? Weekend service?
We have the best pollution control system to meet your needs.	What aspects of your process are polluting the air? What pressure is being brought to bear by the municipality to get you to remedy the situation? What kind of system is best for you?
Our table saws allow for extremely close tolerances.	What kinds of tolerances do you have to have? How are you now assuring those tolerances?
It costs you less, in the long run, to ship your products via our trucks than by any other method.	What's the breakdown of costs to you for shipping your products by your present methods? How does this compare to our costs to you, like: . . . . . . ?
Our pension plan fits in best with most companies' personnel policies and practices.	What is your overall objective in offering fringe benefits to your employees? How does your present pension plan fit in with those objectives? How is your present plan meeting those objectives?

Statements I want to make to my prospect.	Questions I can ask which make *him* interested in what I want to say
Where other factors in a service are equal among various suppliers, reputation is very important.	How does our service rate, in your judgment, compared with our competitors'? How long can you rely on the others' service being as good as ours? How good is their reputation for this as compared to ours?
The greater the order you place now, the longer we shall wait to bill you.	How important is it to you to have more time between invoices from suppliers? What is the proportion of value to you from such use of your money to the cost of tying up a specified amount of money in readily salable stock?
Our lighting system will cut down on burglaries.	What's the rate of burglaries on establishments like yours in this neighborhood? What are you now doing to avoid being burglarized yourself? What do you know about the effectiveness of lighting of the right kind on preventing burglaries?
Our company name has great prestige for those who are associated with it.	What kind of clientele do you want to attract? How much importance do they place on prestige? What do they know about the prestige of our company?
Our fire-extinguisher service people are security cleared.	What are your fire-extinguisher service requirements? How well-equipped are you to handle this with your own people? How important is security in your plant?
Our shellac attracts a market	How much of a shellac clientele

Statements I want to make to my prospect.	Questions I can ask which make *him* interested in what I want to say
you don't now have, which is highly profitable.	do you now have? How much additional profit would such a clientele bring to you?
We want to be a second supplier for you.	Why is it to your disadvantage to have only one supplier? What is your reaction to the other disadvantages, which you haven't mentioned, like: . . . . ? What would you look for in a second supplier?
We make the best canned cocktail preparations in the business.	How busy are your bartenders? How long does it take them to mix the average cocktail? What assurance do you have of uniform quality?
Our cushioning material takes up less space in containers and provides all the protection needed.	What size container do you use? What kind of cushioning do you need? What is the desirable proportion between cushioning space and product space? To what extent are you now achieving this proportion?
Our charter flights provide the best service to your customers.	How many of your customers are interested in having you arrange for them to join charter flights? What elements will convince them that your travel service best meets their wishes? How do your present charter companies stack up to these services: . . . . ?
I want you to use more electricity in your home.	For what home services are you now using electricity? Why aren't you using electricity for these services: . . . . ?

Statements I want to make to my prospect.	Questions I can ask which make *him* interested in what I want to say
Television advertising is much more productive than newspaper advertising.	What kind of coverage do you want for offering your services to the people in this city? How are you now achieving this coverage? What evidence do you have that you are getting effective coverage? How much is your advertising costing you? How much do you know about the effectiveness and cost of the kind of coverage you need, through television advertising?
The best way to be convinced that my transformers are the best in the market is to test them in the user's plant.	What kind of transformer are you now using? How do you know it's the best you can get? How would you go about deciding that a different transformer was better for you?
If a fire takes place in a company, there is additional expense in running it until the necessary repairs have been made.	What are the statistics for fires in your kind of business? How much of your ability to continue producing could be affected by fires? How do you now plan to finance that extra cost in case of fire?
The absence of competition makes for more profitable sales.	How much competition do you now have with your present tool line? How much of a demand is there, in your trade area, for a less-expensive tool? Who is now supplying this need in your trade area?

CAPTURING ATTENTION

Let's get back, now, to the last major point in this chapter.

When you are in the prospect's presence, he is probably still thinking of what had engaged his mind before you came in—or his mind has been roaming or a complete blank.

It's true you've greeted him, introduced yourself or resumed a previous acquaintanceship and sat down. Now you're ready to lead him through a series of thoughts, *under your control,* which will, hopefully, end with his making a firm commitment to whatever you wanted from him.

Things will not happen unless:

- He stops his previous thoughts or listlessness.
- Knows exactly why you're there.
- Is ready to give you his continued, undivided attention.
- Becomes and stays interested in your visit.

My experience convinces me that the most effective way to achieve this is to capture his attention right away and direct it at once to the subject of your call.

This effort on your part belongs in the following sequence of opening activities:

- He knows who you are.
- You've begun to establish or continue rapport.
- You are seated.

NOW YOU MUST SAY OR DO SOMETHING TO GET HIM TO TURN HIS COMPLETE ATTENTION TO WHAT YOU WANT TO DEVELOP

- Then you tell him that you want only to be of service to him and that you, therefore, have to ask him some questions.
- You then begin your questions.

Technique

The best way to attract his attention at the outset is to say and/or do something which combines the following elements:

—It is an arresting statement, question or activity.
—It deals directly with the subject you want to develop.
—It has implicit interest to him.

To accomplish this task, you should plan for it. This means that when you are drawing up your projection of what you are going to do and say during the anticipated call, you should include the device you're going to employ for getting his attention.

If that device includes a tangible object, you must plan on having it ready for effective use, on a surprise basis.

One of the most effective aspects of an attention-getting approach is the use of one or more questions. Occasionally, a question is acceptable for this purpose, if it calls for a *yes* or *no* answer—but only if the question is followed by something else which indicates whether the prospect really understood your question.

Examples

First, I want to give you a complete situation, so you can see the kind of sequence and language you'll want to use. Then, when I present the other examples, I'll not repeat the surrounding words of this first example, since you'll want to select your own.

Case study

I plan on calling on the Purchasing Agent of an electronics assembly plant. The product I want to sell him is my company's spring steel fasteners.

In my general professional reading—which includes *Electronics Monthly,* because so many of my prospects are in the electronics business—I've come across an article which I think I may some day be able to use. I've marked the pages, prepared a card with the subject (alphabetically arranged in my file for this purpose), indicating the name, month and page of the magazine and I've put the publication where I can readily find it.

In preparation for tomorrow's interview, I went through my card file and located a suitable article.

After I've been seated in my prospect's presence, I take out the closed magazine from my briefcase. I hold it up so my prospect can see its title and say to him: "Mr. Jones, have you had a chance to look through this issue of *Electronics Monthly*?"

Now let's see what I say next, depending on his answer.

If he says "yes"	If he says "no"
What did you think of this article (held up by open page) on fasteners for electronics?	Let me read you one sentence from this article (holding it up by open page) on fasteners for electronics.

Then I put the magazine away and say: "That's what I want to talk to you about today. But, since I want to make sure that I am always rendering you the best possible service, I have to ask you some questions. So, here goes."

Now I'm ready to present the variety of samples I mentioned before.

Objective of the call	Attention-getter
Get him to consider switching to a high-strength, low-alloy plate.	Hand him a small piece of such a plate, ask him what he has like it, get it back from him and tell him that you want to discuss with him the benefits of that kind of plate.
Get him to buy my printing ink.	Show him samples of printed matter using several kinds of printing ink, one of which (not identified) is mine. Ask him to tell me the differences in quality he sees. Take the samples back before proceeding.
Get him to stock my company's sports jackets.	Ask him to try one on, get it back from him and put it aside (until I want it again) where it won't distract him.
Get him to try my new beauty aid.	Show him a newspaper article dealing with the increased interest of women in paying attention to their attractiveness.
Get him to experiment with my additive in the feed he manufactures.	Present some government analyses of the effect on cattle of the ingredients I intend to discuss.
Get him to consider using my company's engineering design for his new planned plant.	Show him pictures of plants whose designs we've engineered, in related industries.
Probe whether he is a likely prospect for my mortar.	Ask him to examine a 1-foot section of my mortar bag, which shows the three layers that distinguish my product favorably

Objective of the call	Attention-getter
	from the one he is now using. Ask him what he knows about my kind of mortar bag?
Get him to buy my boiler water treatment system.	Ask him whether we might go, now, to one of the boilers in his plant, before I start my presentation, so I can make it more meaningful to him.
Get him to try my company's fertilizer urea.	Ask him how his latest crop was. Compare his results to statistics I have from a study of those who used a 46% (which happens to be mine, but I don't say so yet) urea.
Get him to buy my paving drill.	Ask him whether he's seen an article in the latest road-paving trade magazine (a copy of which I have) that discusses paving drills.
Get him to stock my home modernizer kit.	Statistics on the volume of sales by stores like his for home-do-it-yourself-repair devices.
Convince a chain-store buyer to try my company's cookies.	Ask him to taste a cookie. Ask him how it compares with the best-tasting cookie he now stocks.
Get him to use our spectrometers in his laboratories.	Show him a list of water pollutants (closely related to his business) identified by our spectrometers.
Get him to try a brand-new kind of carpet for his retail store.	Please examine these samples. Which of them is brand new? What have you read about this kind of carpeting and its enthusiastic acceptance in other parts of this state?

Objective of the call	Attention-getter
Get him to use my polymers in his sponge manufacture.	I'd like you to perform a test. Here are two sponges. Let's soak each of them in this water. What difference in absorption do you note?
Get a doctor to promise to prescribe a new medicine which can be used by adults but is not harmful to children or dogs.	How many of your patients have dogs? Children? What has been your experience with medicines you prescribe for adults which get into the hands of children or are within reach of dogs?
Get a department store buyer to experiment with a new kind of multiple-product display.	Please look at these photos. The dimensions are written at the bottom. How many feet of floor space do you suppose the displays occupy? How many packages do you think one display effectively carries?
Convince him that my company has the best capability of manufacturing catalysts to his custom needs.	Do you buy ready-made catalysts or does your manufacturing process require them to be custom-made?
Get him to use our cigars as sales promotion items for his salesmen's customers.	Do you smoke cigars? (Is there anyone here who does?) I'd like you (him) to smoke this cigar now and give me your (his) opinion of it.
Get him to try new chemical in his processing plant.	I'd like you to see a small experiment. May I use this table?
Familiarize a contractor with my company's capability in building erection.	Please look at these photos. Which of these buildings do you recognize? What have you heard about the economy and solidity of their construction?
Get him to consider using my bolts in his manufacture.	Show him a comparative size-for-size bolt chart.

Objective of the call	Attention-getter
Get him to compare our new rubber product with the one he's now using.	Will you please feel these two pieces of rubber? Which one are you now using? What do you notice about the other one?
Get him to continue to keep my company in mind next time he needs a large quantity of structural steel.	What new buildings are you now bidding on?
Sell him a large order of 16-mm sound projectors for his national sales force, as part of their sales promotion devices.	What do your salesmen now use for an adequate explanation of your process? Let me show you a brief film for a similar sales presentation.
Get him to utilize my connectors in the motors he uses in his machine shop.	How frequently do you have to change connectors in your motors? How long does it take?
Get him to use my fabrics in his clothing manufacture.	I'd like to show you something. See how I stain this fabric with this oil. Now look how easily I wash it off.
Get him to consider buying an additional labelling machine, to work in tandem with his present machine.	Have you seen these figures on cost-per-label production? Please note the two sets of columns, one for a single machine and the other for a tandem operation.
Get him to agree to let my lab process weld areas of his manufacturing process, so we can prove that our process is exactly what he needs.	Show him some samples of the work we've done for others.
Convince him that it's better for him all around to buy a dairy product from us which his chain wants to make in its own facility.	Please look at these comparative cost figures.

Objective of the call	Attention-getter
Get approval from the state to use my company's culvert pipe in its road construction and related activities.	Ask him which states he respects for their culvert work. Show him testimonials from those states for the work we've done for them.
Get him to use our temporary employee service.	Ask him what kinds of problems he has in finding employees on an emergency, temporary basis.
Explain why our establishing another distributor in his city shouldn't hurt his profits.	Show him consumption figures and related maps.
Get him to use my repair service for his vehicles.	Ask him about his problems in getting enough competent, reliable mechanics on a continuing basis.
Get him to let my company present him with the layout for a new canning line.	When did you last check your present cans for the relation between size and shelf space?
Qualify for inclusion on his bidders' list for a cryogenic off-gas treatment system.	Magazine article dealing with the problem my system solves better than the competition.
Find out whether our fiber glass tanks and pipelines are of real benefit to his company, which deals in mining services and supplies.	What kinds of tanks do your customers prefer over all others?
Get him to consider the superiority of buying whiskey brought in from Canada in bulk.	Show him comparative figures of cost and customer acceptance between my product and what he is now buying.
Get more detailed specs before my company can submit a design for his plant's construction.	Show him the list of specs I now have and ask him whether he thinks they are enough for him to be able to make a valid judgment.

Objective of the call	Attention-getter
Find out where we stand on a competitive bid.	Tell him that we've just recently developed a new process which might cut down our cost on services like the one we bid on for him.
Sell a farm distributor on stocking my company's liquid fertilizer, largely because it doesn't give off free NH_3.	Ask him to smell from a small bottle (containing my product) which I am just opening.
Get him to consider installing my bus-door operating equipment in his buses.	Put down before him, right away, the application drawings I've come prepared with, which I'm going to refer to all along.
Make sure that he is carrying the best (for him) stock quantities of my cutlery in each of his outlets.	Put my inventory records (of his stock) in front of him and refer to them, making sure I control their use.
Convince him to convert from citric food acidulants to fumeric food acidulants.	Perform a solubility test (of both kinds of acidulants) right before him.
Convince him to settle his account with us for the quarter.	Chart showing savings from different times of settling accounts.
Get him to put my hotel on his preferred list for meetings, exhibits and/or conventions.	Photos and diagrams showing our facilities.
Get him to use my dental laboratory.	Show him some of the fine work we do.
Try to sell him my company's window-washing service.	Testimonials from companies in his area which he knows and respects.
Sell him my dog-security program for his plant's protection.	Show him statistics on the crime rate in his area and the effect of my kind of protection.

Objective of the call	Attention-getter
Get permission to serve his plant with my mobile catering trucks.	Picture of the truck and cost figures of making other kinds of arrangements for his people.
Come up with an estimate of the cost to him of using my uniform and towel service.	Comparative figures from other companies in his area, as between our price and the cost of doing it in any other way.

Summary

1. Throughout your entire interview you want to make sure that your prospect is always hearing or watching you closely and carefully, and that he is receiving what you say and do with his undivided attention.
2. Never say or do anything in his presence unless you are absolutely sure of that kind of attention.
3. If there are interruptions to that attention, wait until the interruption is over and go back far enough to bring him up to the point where you were just before the interruption.
4. Make sure to say and do exactly what you intend to communicate to him, in such a way that he always considers your ideas valuable and important.
5. In the opening moments of your interview, try to avoid small talk.
6. From your first contact with your prospect, all the way until the last time you have anything to do with him, establish and maintain desirable rapport with him.
7. Among the best ways of establishing and maintaining a prospect's attention and interest are the right kinds of questions.
8. You should carefully plan one or more devices for each of your calls, designed to capture his attention from the very outset, using questions wherever possible.

CHAPTER 5

How to Use Practical Psychology in the Magic Sales Question Technique

TERMS

Let's begin by defining carefully and correctly a number of commonly mis-used and mis-labelled words.

Psychology

Let's begin with that word.

Psychology is either the *study* or the *art* of *human behavior*. It's considered an *art* (rather than a *science*) because it doesn't have all the *exactness* of a science; but it's so close to a science that it can almost be called one.

Human behavior is governed by one's body (anatomy), functioning (physiology), emotions (glandular and otherwise), intellectual capacity (intelligence, "mind," brain plus nervous system), habits, automatic responses, experience and education, environment and stimuli of all kinds (external or internal).

There are only a few *instincts* recognized by psychologists (like hunger, fear, etc.). What we generally call *intuition* is a quick reaction as a result of previous experience, face to face with a situation.

Theory, Generalization, Fact and Opinion

Now let's define those terms.

1. A *theory* is an idea or concept that someone establishes as a result of his thinking and/or experience. Until it is proven to apply always, or in a number of cases accepted by a sufficient number of specialists as true, it stays a theory. Whoever wants to believe it may do so, and it may even work for him. An example of a *theory* is that salesmen are born, not made.

114

- Now, it's true that all salesmen are *born;* they come into the world like everyone else.
- But it's *not* true that anyone is *born* a salesman; he may be born with some (or even all) of the *qualities* that a good salesman needs, but he *develops* into a salesman much later than the day he is born.
- Many people believe the theory stated above. This is their privilege, but it just happens not to be true, as proven by large numbers of specialists in psychology.

But, the approach to closing a sale by offering the prospect two or more alternatives (any one of which is good for the salesman) *started out* as a theory. Someone first got the idea and it turned out to be a very effective method. Now it can no longer be called a *theory*.

Generalization

When an idea, technique, method, thought, etc. is applicable (and effective) in many or most situations, it is called a *generalization* or a general principle. While it might have (and generally does have) its origin in a theory, the idea (etc.) has been proven to be correct, applicable and effective in so many cases that it's worthwhile using it practically all the time. The few exceptions (where it doesn't work) simply require a different or varied approach.

If you have good reason to believe that a technique, method, idea, etc. has been established as *generally* valid, you should try to use it in all cases, unless:

—You have good reason to believe that any one case is an exception, in which situation you will try something else.
—You've tried to apply a general principle in a particular situation, and it turns out that you'd better not pursue it any further at that time. In that eventuality, you'll try something else.

An example of a generalization is this: Asking questions in a sales interview is more effective than making statements without asking questions.

This general principle started out as a theory. Broad experience has proven that it's a valid generalization.

Fact vs. opinion

All thoughts, reactions, statements and situations, etc. can be classified as either *facts, opinions* or *faith.* I won't go into the question of *faith* in this book, because in its true definition it isn't applicable to my treatment. Of course, if *faith* is used by anyone as a synonym for *confidence* (or something similar), I prefer to deal with the other word (e.g.: *confidence*) and not discuss the word *faith* at all.

That leaves us with *fact* vs. *opinion.*

A *fact* is *that which is,* regardless of whether any one person knows that something is a fact or agrees that it is a fact. Everything else is *opinion.* In a later chapter, I'll develop this distinction more fully. In this chapter, I introduce the term only as a prelude to some additional statements I want to make below about psychology.

Two More Terms

1. The word *practice (application)* may mean several things. Here I use it to mean the repetition of an activity (or series of statements/questions) which have proven to be valid as a general principle. For example:

   Generalization: A salesman must take a positive step to *close* a sale or he may not get the order.

   Practice   At the right moment in any interview, ask a
   (Application):   question or make a statement which will induce the prospect to make a firm commitment to you along the lines you wish.

2. *Common sense:* Different people use this term to mean different things. Unfortunately, the term in itself means only what anyone wants it to mean, and is therefore an inefficient way in which to communicate. I suggest that you say *intelligence, experience, education* or *judgment,* depending on what you mean.

ROLE OF PSYCHOLOGY IN SELLING

All selling consists of a series of *stimuli* (hopefully initiated by you, although it may be by the prospect) which are intended to induce the prospect to make the *response* you want—a firm commitment *today* to do or say what you want him to do or say.

Human behavior is also, largely, a matter of stimulus/response. It has long been proven that human beings *respond* in certain ways to specific *stimuli.*

Now, here's a sequence of thoughts I'd like to present to you:

1. Selling is largely a matter of "stimulus/response." You have to provide those stimuli which will lead to the kind of response you want from the prospect.
2. Human behavior is largely a matter of stimulus/response.
3. Psychology is largely a study (or the art) of stimulus/response.
4. The stimuli/responses in psychology are much broader than just selling, but

every stimulus/response involved in selling is part of the overall study/art of stimulus/response in psychology.

5. Therefore, the more you know about psychological stimulus/response in general, the more you'll know about stimulus/response when you have to apply it to selling.

6. Therefore, a strong knowledge and wise use of psychology is of great value to you in salesmanship.

What Should You Believe?

You're a pretty sophisticated person. You don't believe everything you see or hear. And that's good. So, why should you believe that psychology is "all important" in making things happen in selling?

HOW VALID PSYCHOLOGICAL PRINCIPLES ARISE

As a general rule, here's how a reputable psychologist functions:

- He studies what all other reputable psychologists have done and said.
- He thinks about one or more aspects of human behavior that interest him and observes that behavior on a broad base of experience.
- He finally develops a theory of human behavior which is in some respect a variation of what all of his predecessors have come up with.
- He performs large numbers of experiments, following well-accepted rules for such experiments, to see whether his theory is valid.
- If he finds it to be valid, he reports it to all the other psychologists (along with the details of his experiments) in articles (or other publications) and/or by presentations at meetings of psychologists.
- The other reputable psychologists try out his theory, either by their own experiments or otherwise.
- When a large number of reputable psychologists agree that his theory is a valid principle of human behavior, they accept it as such and it becomes established as a general principle applied by most, if not all of them.

Your Choice

Now let's see how this applies to you.

- —You want to sell as effectively as you can, all the time.
- —Your effectiveness depends in large measure on how you provide the stimuli which will lead to the responses you want.
- —Reputable psychologists have already established sure-fire methods for obtaining a particular response that you may want.
- —Your own way of doing this may or may not be as good as their proven approaches.

If you don't at least *know* what they've come up with, you may be using an inferior technique when an effective one is available.

This leads up to my recommendation to you to:

- Study as much as you can (or refresh yourself on your previous studies) of psychology.
- Learn as much as you can about how most effectively to get the kinds of responses you want from people.
- Apply this to your selling stimuli, in addition to your own proven techniques.

How to Make Things Happen with Applied Psychology

Now I'm going to take up the major aspects of selling and show you how to apply relevant principles of valid psychology to those efforts.

PSYCHOLOGY AND SELLING

I'm going to present to you a series of guidelines on this subject, describing a selling step, showing the application of valid psychology to it and giving examples of the application of this from my own experience.

Essential steps in effective selling	Valid principles of applicable psychology	Examples from selling situations I've participated in
The salesman must fully believe that the combination of his company, his product or service and himself is unbeatable for that prospect.	In a true selling situation, the prospect, at the outset, is not yet convinced that he should do what the salesman wants him to. If the salesman is not fully convinced that his own objective is absolutely the best thing that the prospect can do for his own good, this will definitely be communicated to the prospect. The salesman's own doubts or	In the thousands of contacts I've had with salesmen from different kinds of businesses and companies (individually or in groups), I've heard them ask me: "What should I do when I'm face to face with a prospect where my company doesn't back me up" or "my product/service is no better than the competition's," and "even higher-priced"? To them I always say:

Essential steps in effective selling	Valid principles of applicable psychology	Examples from selling situations I've participated in
	uncertainties will feed the prospect's initial doubts or indifference and will interfere materially with his decisions.	"Consider the combination of yourself with your company and the product/service. If that combination isn't superior, in your mind, to anything in the competition for that prospect, you'll lose the sale to the man who does have that confidence."
You must always have a firm, valid objective.	Every purpose that a person has is more readily attainable if the aspirant's objective is clearly known to both people involved in the purpose.	I've seen salesman after salesman flounder in an interview because neither person knew what was being sought after.
Always plan what you want to say and do during the interview.	If you don't seem to know what you want to say during the visit, the prospect will either lose interest or take control of the conversation, in order to turn you down or accede only to a portion of what he really can use from what you have to offer.	The majority of salesmen I've seen in action start right in with the same pitch they always use, without having anticipated the differences that may exist (in that particular prospect's needs) from the needs expressed in the standard pitch.
Have your sales kit in good order and easy to use.	If you want to find something to show a prospect, and can't find it at once, the prospect will not only lose interest but also confidence in you.	I was making a joint call with a furniture salesman (of a department store chain) who said to the buyer that his company had a brand-new line of

Essential steps in effective selling	Valid principles of applicable psychology	Examples from selling situations I've participated in.
		upholstered furniture which was just what they needed. He then said he wanted the buyer to see some fine photos. It took him two full minutes to find them in his sales kit.
Decide in each case whether to make an appointment in advance.	Unless your company's policy (or the prospect's policy) insists on appointments (or you would have to travel a great distance to get there), you're better off without an appointment, because you don't give the prospect a chance to say *no* over the phone.	I heard a salesman phone for an appointment. The prospect insisted on hearing the sales presentation on the phone. The salesman never did get to see him.
Don't tell your story to anyone who doesn't materially affect the decision you seek, no matter how easy it is to see that person.	If you find it difficult to get in to see the one man you must see, at any one time, and an intermediary tells you that he's been asked to get your story (so *he* can tell it to the real prospect), you lose out as follows: a. If the intermediary actually does tell the story to the prospect, he either cannot or doesn't want to tell it the way you would.	Every time I've been in that situation, I've handled it like this: *Intermediary:* Mr. Jones has asked me to find out what you want, so I can tell him. He's too busy to see you. *W.W.:* That's very kind of both of you. Tell me, what role do you personally play in the final decision to buy? (Answer vague, but I'm convinced it's *none.*) In that case, I'll tell you

Essential steps in effective selling	Valid principles of applicable psychology	Examples from selling situations I've participated in.
	b. He probably will spoil your sale for you. c. The prospect may feel that you've already had your chance, and not give you another.	what you can do for me. Find out when I can meet with both you *and* Mr. Jones. (And I absolutely refrain from telling him anything else, while trying to be as polite and respectful as possible. If necessary, I'll leave and start all over again with Mr. Jones at a later, more suitable time.)
Don't start to present your story unless you're in the best physical situation.	If you are standing behind a barrier, have to chase after a moving prospect, can't sit down, etc., you're at a psychological disadvantage—demeaned, or not subject to good attention, or harried and/or hurried. Better wait until you're in a good situation, even if you have to come back at a later time.	On one occasion, I wanted to see a Sales Manager. He came to the swinging gate between the office and the reception room, and asked: "What can I do for you?" I replied: "You can ask me into your office so I can spread some charts out on your desk to show you how to increase your sales by 25%." And he did.
Establish and maintain rapport all the time.	As I've already told you, a person is more apt to be receptive to someone he enjoys being with than to someone with whom he feels either ill-at-ease or bored.	I've seen prospects "all ears" to salesmen whose appearance, manner and message please them. On the other hand, I've noticed how prospects have been positively unreceptive to men who:

Essential steps in effective selling	Valid principles of applicable psychology	Examples form selling situations I've participated in
		are sloppy or garish in their appearance; were as dull as could be; talked so low they couldn't be heard; etc.
Don't interrupt yourself or divert the prospect's attention through your own acts or statements.	It's difficult enough to get your prospect to pay close attention to what you are saying and doing when you are careful to provide proper continuity, without yourself contributing to this distraction.	I've seen salesmen lose the desired continuity by their own mistakes, like: suddenly giving in to the desire to smoke, in the midst of developing a complicated idea; telling a joke of which he is reminded by something the prospect said; falling into the trap of continuing along the lines of the prospect's digression.
Establish and maintain prospect attention and interest all along.	Unless a prospect is continually attentive, he will miss the continuity so necessary for conviction. If he isn't interested, he won't even listen.	(See the preceding chapter on attention and interest.)

THE PSYCHOLOGY OF PRESENTATION

Now let's see how valid principles of psychology can and should be applied to the presentation itself, to make things happen.

Here are the basic concepts:

1. If it is a true *selling* situation (as distinguished from one where the salesman simply takes the prospect's order to the extent that the prospect wants to give it), the prospect has (before you approach him) one or more (if not all) of the following frames of mind:

> a. Here I was minding my own business (or taking care of something important to me) when this guy barged in on me (even if he had

an appointment) and prevented me from doing what I wanted to do.

> You can avoid any bad effects from such an attitude, if it exists, by good rapport and a valuable (to him) message.

b. I don't like salesmen in general, and I particularly don't like this salesman and/or his company/product/ service.

> Be the kind of salesman he does like and, if he has had a wrong attitude toward you, undo it through the right kind of rapport.

c. I'm perfectly happy with what I now have and don't want or need what he has to offer, which is no better than (or not as good as) what I now have.

> You've got to make him *unhappy* with what he now has and prove to him that your entire *package* (your company, your product/service and you) is the best he can find anywhere—for *him*.

d. I don't have very much time to spend with him.

> If this is really true, spend the little time he has convincing him to see you at a later date when he has all the time you'll need. If he really does have enough time, be so interesting and valuable to him that he'll *want* to spend enough time with you.

e. If I change from what I've been using all along I'm going to feel silly, stupid or embarrassed, because I wasn't as smart before as this guy tells me I should now be; and I won't like him because he made me feel that way.

> Be as polite and subtle as you can. Try to make him feel that nobody could expect him to have known about the existence or superiority of your product/service. But don't kid yourself—if he doesn't realize that what you have to offer (all around) is better than what he is now using, he won't buy from you.

2. The kind of reaction he will make to you, and his decisions, will depend as much on his makeup as on you and your package. Every human being has certain reactions to others, which affect the way in which he will cooperate with those others.

    a. Here are some examples of the characteristics of prospects, which will determine how they will react to you and your message:

       • Superiority Complex: Must prevail in any conversation and must never have to admit he can do any wrong. By the proper use of questions, you can get him to tell you what you want to tell him so he can look important to himself.

For example: In your wide experience, what kind of security system would you say is the most reliable?

- Vacillating: Unwilling to make decisions. Ask him how urgent is his need for improving the situation about which you are talking, and show him how his immediate acceptance of your proposition will best meet that urgency.

- Brash, Impatient, Domineering: Must dominate every situation and has no interest in what anyone else says but himself. Use questions to get him to tell you his situation relative to your proposition, and show him how what you have to offer best meets that situation.

- Stubborn, Loyal, Inflexible: Almost impossible to get him to change and unwilling to hurt the feelings of the present supplier. Use questions to get him to state that he needs what you have to offer. Then ask him whether he knows of any reason for not benefiting from your product/service, which is more important than such benefit.

- Vain, Self-Centered, Egotistical: Must shine and feel that he's the most important, successful person in the circles in which he travels. Try to relate your questions to answers which will make him feel that he will come out brilliantly when he accepts your offer.

- Evasive, Dilatory, Slippery: Refuses to be pinned down and tries not to say what he's actually thinking. Ask the kinds of questions which will force him to show his hand, like: Exactly how many times a month do you have to change that filter?

- Taciturn, Uncommunicative, Unfriendly: Will sit and look at you without saying a word. Ask one question after another until he answers you.

- Talkative, Wandering, Digressive: Won't let you get a word in edgewise and won't stick to the point. Interrupt him as often as necessary, saying something like: "Apropos of what you've just said, . . . ," and then asking a question you've planned all along.

- Opinionated, Cocksure, Arrogant: Thinks he knows it all. Say: "You're absolutely right. That's why I wanted your opinion. What do *you* think of . . .?" Then ask a question you've planned all along.

b. The psychological principle involved here is:

—You must constantly be aware of the fact that every prospect probably has one or more quirks which can affect his reactions to you and his decision.

—You have to find out what those quirks are just as soon as possible, as a result of the continuing qualification of that prospect and your previous contacts with him.

—You have to give in to the quirk, or take advantage of it, at the same time that you continue to advance your own cause. Don't try to change his attitudes in general and don't let him know that you are aware of those qualities. Don't in any way show that you are displeased with his habits.

3. *The psychology of questions:*   Psychologists have proven beyond a doubt that the following are universal facts about effective communication:

   a. A man who responds to a question (other than *yes* or *no*) will thereby always reveal:

- Whether he has heard.
- Whether he is interested.
- His degree of receptivity.
- Just what he has understood.
- Whether he agrees, disagrees or has reservations.
- His acceptance or rejection.
- Where he'd like to go from there.

   b. The proper number, kinds and sequence of questions are the most effective way of:

- Guiding his thinking.
- Involving him.
- Leading him from one step to the next (proper) one.
- Getting him to sell himself.

Now let's take a number of examples, from my own experience, (as a trainer, consultant or salesman), of questions that were asked (or to be asked) in sales interviews, which led to desirable sales development for *psychological* reasons.

Sales situations	Questions asked	Psychological reasons for, and effects of, the questions
The prospect wants to continue to use his present warehouseman because he's closer.	1. How much time generally elapses between your requesting a delivery and your receipt of it? 2. Our warehouse is	If the 20 miles of greater distance was important, I wasn't going to make my sale. I was better off finding that out before I spent too much time with

Sales situations	Questions asked	Psychological reasons for, and effects of the questions
	only 20 miles farther away from you than his. How much difference will that generally make in your ability to get delivery when you need it?	him. By getting him to tell me that he required a specific lead time for delivery (which, as I had suspected, could easily be met by me), I was able to ask my next question, whose answer convinced him (he, himself, being the convincer) that my greater distance was not a factor. I was then able to get his complete and undivided attention, and his receptivity to my main rationale for his using my superior warehouse.
The prospect likes to have his office windows cleaned in a certain way (which is different from—and inferior to—mine).	1. What requirements do you have for the way you like the windows washed? 2. Why do you set . . . as a requirement?	By asking him to state the requirements, I got him to clear *his* mind and satisfy mine. Then I was able to take those requirements which I felt were unessential and get him to initiate the process (by giving his reasons for them) of showing him how they (different from mine) unnecessarily stood in the way of using my superior service.
One of the strongest reasons for buying my company's product	1. How frequently do you have follow-up problems with your present equipment? 2. How much of your	Before playing up the fact that my company had many qualified technicians, I had to find out whether he

Sales situations	Questions asked	Psychological reasons for, and effects of the questions
is the large number of highly trained technicians we have for helping our customers with follow-up problems.	own technicians' time is taken up in effecting that follow-up? 3. How quickly can you get your present supplier to send you qualified technicians when you need them?	had any and how much this cost him. When I found that he didn't have enough, I wanted to find out how well his present supplier served him in this way. When it was revealed that they didn't have enough, I was in the strong position of playing up one of the best reasons for buying my equipment.
The prospect had to have an assembly which would always work properly. This depends mostly on the excellence of each component.	1. What percentage of failures can you tolerate in your assemblies? 2. In the breakdowns you've been having in your assemblies, what proportion have you been able to trace to your present components?	It was essential to focus his attention on the periodic failures in his present assemblies and get him to realize/admit that this was costing him money and, perhaps, customers. Then, since the salesman wanted to sell him components, it was necessary to get the prospect to realize that good components led to good assemblies. Then it would be easy to show how our components should be bought, because they filled that bill.
Prompt pickup and delivery of laboratory samples were the salesman's	1. What kind of timetable do you offer your prospects? 2. Is it crucial to them to get this kind of	There was no question that our service was more expensive to the prospect, but none could touch us in

Sales situations	Questions asked	Psychological reasons for, and effects of the questions
strongest point, although his price was higher.	fast service or doesn't it matter to them? 3. How high are they willing to go in fees for that kind of service?	speedy service. If this didn't mean anything to the prospect, we might as well not waste any time with him, since that was the only reason he could go for the higher price. If we could make him see that he could charge more and still get more customers (wanting our kind of speed), we could sell him even at the higher price.
The contractor is accustomed to using gas heating in his buildings, and we want to sell him electric heating.	1. What advantages does gas heating bring you and your occupants? 2. What disadvantages or shortcomings does gas heating have?	I have to overcome the inertia of his practice of using gas heat. By asking about the advantages of gas heat, I'll be able to show that electric heat has them too. By asking about the disadvantages of gas heat, I make him receptive to electric heat (which overcomes those disadvantages).
A customer is purchasing only some of the supplier's lines, not buying others which he can definitely use.	1. How many of the items on this list of our products are you now buying from someone else? 2. Which of the ones you are buying from them are superior in any way to ours? 3. Why aren't you buying them from us?	Instead of telling him which products he isn't buying from us, I get him to tell me, so there's no doubt about it. Then, I get him to tell me which of them, if any, are superior to mine. For those which aren't, I put him in the position of trying to

Sales situations	Questions asked	Psychological reasons for, and effects of the questions
		find a good reason why he shouldn't buy them from us. Then I can point out to him the advantages of dealing with someone he can rely on, with a minimum of duplication of ordering, paying, etc.
I want the prospect to buy my appliances, though more costly, because I'll carry the bulk of his inventory.	1. To what extent can you carry a sufficient inventory for immediate delivery to all your customers? 2. What does it cost you to carry the inventory, have the appliances sent to you and then deliver them to the customers?	I want him to realize that he can't carry a complete inventory anyway. Then I want him to see that it costs him more the way he now does it. He's then ready to understand that the additional cost is less than his present method and my way is at least as speedy as his.
My brand name will sell more of his product line than a less well-known one.	1. What induces people to come into your store to buy refrigerators? 2. What are your present suppliers doing to help you turn them over more frequently? 3. How much is the promotion costing *you*?	Here's the thinking I want him to do: People come to me to buy refrigerators if they know that I have the kind they want. The better the promotion, the better they'll know about me and my store as the best place to come to. The competition doesn't do a satisfactory job on promotion, so I have to spend my own money on this, thus decreasing my margin. Now he's ready to appreciate the bene-

Sales situations	Questions asked	Psychological reasons for, and effects of the questions
		fit to him of my promotions.
He is better off sticking to his business (wholesale meats) and letting me take care of his trucking.	1. How many men do you employ in maintaining, controlling and driving your trucks? 2. What does this cost you a year? 3. How much of this could you invest in your main business for greater profit?	Get him to realize that by doing his own trucking, he is using men and money. Show him how much less expensive this would be if we handled his trucking. Show him how he could devote more time and money to the business he knows best, and from which, therefore, he can derive more profit.
I want to design a tailored visual for use by his salesmen.	1. How do you get your men to present your service in the sequence *you* find most effective? 2. How do they keep the prospect's attention? 3. Is your present visual a sales promotion piece or a sales aid?	One of the biggest problems sales managers have is to get their men to follow the right sequence of ideas. Another is that most salesmen lack dynamic, attention-getting skills. If you already have a visual, is it really an aid? Now he's ready to listen to my reasoning that he needs a *sales-aid* visual tailored for him and his men.
I want to get him to buy my abrasives because they will save him money.	1. What kind of abrasives are you now using in your machine? 2. How long do they last?	I want him to concentrate on the fact that his machine uses abrasives. Then I want him to recall the frequency with which he has to

Sales situations	Questions asked	Psychological reasons for, and effects of the questions
	3. What is the total cost to you of buying, storing and changing abrasives?	change them. Finally, I want him to realize how much it costs him to use the kind of shorter-lasting abrasives he now buys. Then he is psychologically ready to accept the fact that my abrasives, no matter how high-priced they at first seem, cost him less.
I want a hospital administrator to give me enough information about his credit and collection practices so I can tailor a program for him, whereby we manage the whole activity for his hospital.	1. How many people under you work on credit and collection? 2. How frequently do you find yourself without enough qualified people for all of your credit and collection activities? 3. How much does your whole credit and collection operation cost you? 4. How much are you losing in unwise credit decisions by some of your people? 5. How much are you losing in delayed collections? 6. How much do you lose per year in unpaid bills?	I have to get him psychologically set to realize that he is not doing so well in handling his own credit and collection activities. Since I get him to focus his concern on the reasons why he is not getting satisfactory results, I can then take one reason at a time and show him how we can do better, because that's *all* we do—we have steadier employment (we pay more) and greater efficiency and effectiveness.
I want to con-	1. How do you now	I want him to realize

Sales situations	Questions asked	Psychological reasons for, and effects of the questions
vince him that my company's computer-controlled inventory system assures an efficient inventory control for him at no inventory-control cost.	keep your drug and sundries inventory up to the minute? 2. How much does this cost you? 3. How frequently do you find yourself unable to supply a retailer on time?	that he has too many items to be able to control his inventory effectively without a computer. I also want him to understand what the undesirable effects of this will be on his business. Then he's ready to accept my demonstration: By buying from my manufacturing house, he gets my inventory system completely at his disposal.
I want to convince him to sign a contract with my company to service his fire extinguishers.	1. How many fire extinguishers do you have in your plant? 2. Where are they located? 3. What is your current schedule for inspecting and servicing them? 4. What do you use for spares while one or more of your extinguishers is out of service? 5. How many men do you have working on this activity? 6. Is it full time or in addition to other duties? 7. What's the total cost to you of the whole activity? 8. What has been your	I want to get him thinking that: a. he has enough fire extinguishers, sufficiently far apart, to make servicing them time-consuming; b. his schedule may not be up to standard because the task is greater than he can provide men for; c. he has to maintain spares; d. he isn't getting maximum/optimum use of men with more than one set of duties. I then get him to realize that his less than desirable system costs more than it has to. I want, also, to show him that it is less efficient than it has to be. He is now psychologically ready

Sales situations	Questions asked	Psychological reasons for, and effects of the questions
	record of success in maintenance and service?	to consider a better and less costly approach.
I want the Personnel Manager of a large, national company to use my company's executive search facilities in getting candidates for positions they are seeking to fill.	1. How many management and skilled technical positions are you now seeking to fill? 2. What are their categories? 3. What avenues for search have you been employing? 4. How long does it take you, on the average, to find what you think is the right person? 5. How much does this generally cost you? 6. What degree of success have you had in hiring people who turned out to be good executives after three to six months?	Unless he has a sufficient number of positions to fill, my approach should be to get him to engage us on an interim basis, instead of the overall basis I seek. I must get him to realize that he doesn't have enough satisfactory sources for his recruitment, that it takes him too long to find suitable candidates and that it costs him at least as much to do it his way as mine, and with less success. Only then is he ready to receive my suggestions with a positive reaction.

THE PSYCHOLOGY OF PROOF

In a later chapter, I shall explain how best to follow up on the answers of the prospect, to the questions you ask, in order to clinch the sale. But here I want to develop the psychology behind that approach.

Rationale

When you ask questions whose answers reveal that you are still on the right track, here's what's happening psychologically:

- The prospect is consciously thinking of the subject on which you want him to concentrate.

- He is expressing and feeling a desire or need/lack for a product, service or intermediate activity which you want him to be eager for.
- He is not yet aware that your questions must lead to his expressed need or desire for what only you can offer him to his complete satisfaction.
- He is ready to accept wholeheartedly anything which will meet that need or desire, because you have made him either:
    - —Dissatisfied with the inferior situation in which he finds himself because he's been buying from the competition; or
    - —Restless because he doesn't have at all what he now realizes he wants or needs.

Clincher

Now you say something to this effect:

1. You have said that you're looking for. . . .
2. I'm very happy to be able to tell you that that's exactly what I have to offer you.
3. What's more, my solution to your situation is the best that you can find anywhere.

Now, from a psychological standpoint, he's ready to believe you and accept your offer wholeheartedly. But, again psychologically, he's still in the habit of insisting on proof that what you've said is absolutely true.

It's for this reason that you now have to prove that what you've said is so. That's the subject we'll develop in a later chapter dealing with proof.

THE PSYCHOLOGY OF THE MAKE-HAPPEN CLOSE

The psychology of the close is that it is not enough for *you* to *believe* that the prospect has gone along with you in the conviction that you've been successful. He has to say or do something which shows both you and him that *he* is thus convinced.

Commitment

So, from a psychological standpoint, the salesman must always take a positive step to get the prospect to make a firm commitment, before the salesman leaves, to do what the salesman wants him to, even if the actual doing will take place later.

And, the salesman must get this firm commitment in such form that there is little likelihood of backing down—a signed order; a definite promise to accept a sample and try it; an immediate telephone call to someone to follow up on the commitment; etc.

Philosophy of Closing

Those salesmen who don't use the magic formula of questioning generally view the close as a separate step in the sales visit, after what they call the *presentation*. The technique I've been developing in this book takes fuller/better advantage of the psychology of prospect decision by:

1. Making the *entire* interview one continuous closing effort.
2. Making it unnecessary to engage in a formal, obvious closing effort.
3. Still saying something at the end which forces the right kind of willing, affirmative decision.

I have been illustrating, all along, how this is done. But in the chapter on making things happen, I'll round out the concept and the practice.

THE PSYCHOLOGY OF HANDLING OBJECTIONS

Here, too, I shall have a chapter, later, on objections. But in the present treatment, I want to explain the *psychology* which underlies both the objection and its handling.

Reasons for Objections

There are a number of causes for objections, obstacles, questions and delaying tactics, chief among them being:

A. The prospect doesn't really want to spend any (more) time with you and is too polite to ask you to leave.
B. He feels himself being persuaded to your view but doesn't want to be won over, at least not yet.
C. He really doesn't understand something, or its implications.
D. He feels that what you are offering is not the best thing for him.
E. He is not in a position to make a decision now.

Preventing Objections from Arising

The best way to avoid the psychological phenomenon of the objection is to anticipate it and answer it before he either thinks of it or says anything about it. The question technique is ideal for this because by the very nature of your questions and his answers, you are guided in what to say and do next.

Handling Objections

If, however, despite all that you have anticipated, he still raises an objection, sound psychology requires a speedy analysis by you of his *real* objection (regardless of what he says) and your reaction to that analysis. As a general rule, he is really saying one or more of the following things:

- *Go away, you're bothering me.* You should reply to this by saying something like: "That's very interesting. I'd like to discuss this point later." You can thus pay him the attention he wants, avoid being diverted when it isn't really necessary and handle the matter when *you* are ready for it.
- *I don't want to be persuaded.* To this you can say "Yes, but . . .", and go right on as though he hadn't said anything at all. This satisfies him that you're heeding him but, again, prevents him from diverting you.
- *Hold on! I have a serious objection.* This you have to tackle with full attention, right then and there, and completely overcome. There is no method that can even touch the question for this purpose.

The entire approach to handling objections will be developed fully in a later chapter.

PSYCHOLOGY OF THE FOLLOW-UP

When you have finished saying and doing everything you intended to, in pursuit of your objective, you must immediately do two things— from a psychological viewpoint:

1. Make provision for whatever follow-up is called for (another appointment; something you will send him; something he will send you; etc.). The psychology behind this is that if you intend to continue to call on him (for whatever objective), you want him to know that right then and there and begin at once to be receptive and cooperate with you in the planning for that follow-up.
2. Thank him, say *goodbye* and quickly get out of there before he changes his mind about what he's promised to do or say.

Summary

1. Psychology is the study or art of human behavior.
2. Human behavior revolves around stimulus and response.
3. Selling consists of a salesman's providing a prospect with the stimuli which the salesman knows will yield the desired prospect response.
4. Psychology has clearly defined the kinds of stimuli needed for specific responses.
5. Therefore, the more you know about and practice the valid principles of psychology, the better you'll be able to know what responses you have a right to expect and what stimuli are needed to provoke those responses.
6. Asking the right questions at the right time, and correctly interpreting the answers, depends to a large extent on how well you know and apply the principles of psychology.
7. Since asking questions is the most effective way of selling, it lends itself quite naturally to valid, practical psychology, which is so essential to any kind of selling.

CHAPTER 6

How to Use Practical Logic in the Magic Sales Question Technique

As you well know, selling is a process of *convincing*. There are all kinds of different ways of accomplishing this. My experience has shown, as I've been saying all along, that asking questions of the right kind—in the right way and in the right sequence—is the most effective technique for convincing a prospect to do what you want him to.

But this magic formula for making things happen is based on a magic discovery made a long time ago by someone else, a system called *logic*. It is the practical use of logic in the question technique that I shall discuss in the present chapter.

MAKING THINGS HAPPEN WITH FACTS

Before I get into an explanation and discussion of logic, let's analyze once more, although from a different angle, the concept of fact.

Re-Definition

A *fact* is that which is. If a certain situation is a fact, it is one regardless of whether:

- A particular individual or group of individuals knows that it is a fact.
- Anyone involved is ready to accept that it is a fact.

If, however, I know a fact which it is important for me to communicate to someone else, I may have to:

—Make him aware of that fact, something he hadn't known until then.
—Convince him that it *is* a fact, if he doubts it.

If I don't succeed in either or both of those efforts, my fact may be of little use to me. Now let's apply this to the selling situation.

At the beginning of each sales call, one of several situations already exists:

- The prospect previously decides what he wants, agrees that what you have to offer is what he wants and is ready to do what you want him to. This is the process of order-taking and should be grabbed at by you whenever it's present. It is not, however, *selling* and requires no particular technique. Also, when you've taken the order, you should consider whether, while you're there, you can *sell* him anything additional which he might need or want. And, if you can, hop to it.

- You start to sell for your objective, and the prospect immediately becomes aware that what you are offering is indeed what he needs or wants. You don't then, have to convince him of your facts. All you have to do is present them to him and follow up with the necessary steps.

- The prospect understands what you are saying but he is not yet convinced that what you are offering him is really the best package for his needs or wants. This is the only *real* selling situation. This is the area where you will succeed only if:

    —You marshal and properly present all the relevant facts.

    —You convince him that the facts you presented to him are indeed *facts*.

Once you accomplish this, you've got it made. You need only make the additional statements which externalize and verbalize the fact that he is ready to close—to do or say what you want him to as a firm commitment, accepting your proposition/offer.

PROVING FACTS

Let's review, now, what you have to prove to a prospect in a true selling situation.

A. You need/want this particular type of product/service.

B. The combination I offer (my product/service, my company and I, myself) not only fully meets those needs/wants, but it meets them better than anything the competition has to offer. And if there is or was no competition, that's all the more reason why I'm confident that what I have to offer you is *exactly* and *fully* what you need/want.

C. You are much better off taking the firm steps *now* (needed for you to avail yourself *now* of my offer) so you can have at the earliest possible, *necessary* moment what you need/want.

D. So, here's what we'll do: . . . . (Steps leading to an immediate commitment, a firm one by him, accepting your proposition.)

Now let's see what methods of proof are available to you.

How to Prove Facts

There are two basic ways in which you can prove to another person that what you know to be a fact *is* a fact, when he is not yet ready to accept that it is a fact.

1. You demonstrate to him that it is a fact through one or more of the five senses (sight, hearing, touch, taste, smell). And this, in turn, divides itself into two types of demonstrations:

    a. You can demonstrate it right then and there. For example:
    - Look at the colors of this display and note how attractive they are.
    - Listen to this commercial and see how catchy the tune is.
    - Feel the softness of this fabric.
    - Taste this cookie and see how pleasant it is to eat.
    - Smell this gas and note that it is odorless.

    Whenever It Is Important to Prove a Fact on the Spot Which Lends Itself to That Kind of Demonstration, Use It Immediately

    b. You can't demonstrate it right then and there, but you could at a different place or time. Under such circumstances, never try to prove (what is disputed or disbelieved) at a time or place inappropriate for such proof, something which *can* be effectively proven at a different time or place. When you are faced with such a situation:
    - Acknowledge it.
    - Say that you know you can prove it, though not here and now.
    - Try to get the prospect to let you prove it at a different (specific) time and/or place.
    - Bring that time or place about as quickly as possible.
    - Prove it at that time/place.

Here are some examples of what I mean about making things happen with facts.

What you're trying to prove through one or more of the senses	Why you can't effectively prove it right then and there	When and where (and how) you can more effectively prove it
How clean your window	It wasn't economical for you to bring a win-	Either have him come with you to a location

What you're trying to prove through one or more of the senses	Why you can't effectively prove it right then and there	When and where (and how) you can more effectively prove it
washers can clean his windows, and in how little time.	dow-washer along with you on that call because you couldn't have anticipated that he would be ready for that kind of demonstration.	where you are now doing a job or arrange for one of your washers to come to him at a good time.
How relatively noiseless your machinery is when it's running.	You can't bring the entire machine to his location and run it for him there.	Have him come to either your model plant or that of a satisfied customer.
How smooth to the touch your coats are, all of them.	You didn't know, when you were getting ready to visit him, that he'd want to feel one or all of the many different kinds of coats you sell, so you didn't take them along.	Set up another time when you can bring them along or invite him to come to your showroom.
How tasty your entire line of catered foods is.	It would be impractical to take them all along. Besides, much of the tastiness depends on the freshness of the foods right after preparation.	Invite him to either your model kitchen or an establishment/customer now using the line.
How relatively odorless is the exhaust from a complicated piece of machinery.	You can't set the machinery up there just for that demonstration.	Invite him to either your model plant or one belonging to a satisfied customer.
How efficient is the office layout you want to design for him.	Drawings, photos and statistics aren't satisfying him.	Invite him to an office now using your design.

2. You have to *reason* with him, because you can't effectively demonstrate/prove your fact (for whatever cause), in order to get him to understand and agree that what you say is really so.

Now I'm ready to develop with you in great detail what is the most effective way of accomplishing this reasoning.

Recapitulation

Let's review, first, what we're trying to accomplish, and why we must use a *rational* approach rather than the demonstrative one explained above.

- I am convinced that what I have to offer my prospect is exactly what he needs.
- I want to convince *him* that it is a *fact* that what I have to offer him is exactly what he needs or wants, better than anything else he can get anywhere.
- The nature of my fact is such that I cannot effectively demonstrate (there and then, or anywhere/anytime) its validity by appealing to one or more of the five senses.
- I must, therefore, so explain and develop my fact through reasoning, that he:
    - Understands exactly what I am saying.
    - Realizes that it is absolutely true.
    - Recognizes that it is exactly what he needs/wants.
    - Is so impelled to give me the firm commitment I desire, that he will do or say whatever I want him to in order to close that visit successfully.

Now all that remains is to see what kind of reasoning I need to use for this objective of mine, and how I can make most effective use of it.

REASONING AND LOGIC

There are a number of ways that this kind of reasoning can be attempted, but experience has shown that the most effective way is through what is called *logic*. Logic is a very effective means for establishing a fact, and it can be effectively used to make things happen in selling.

The Role of Emotions

Before I go any further into the subject of logic, I want to comment, briefly, on the subject of emotions.

In some selling situations, it may be necessary to appeal to the prospect's emotions. If that is so in any particular case, then by all means do what your company's policies (or your own valid experience) call for. Just make sure that you are using the emotions *only* where that is the most effective (or only) way to accomplish your objective.

I don't, however, advocate emotional selling, and therefore don't devote any time to its development in this book. Consequently, what I am saying is:

- Use reasoning whenever and wherever a demonstration won't work.
- Inject as much reasoning as you can when you feel that you must appeal to the emotions.

Thus, if you learn how to employ the best kind of reasoning—logic—you can use it effectively whenever it is called for.

Facets of Logic

Many wise men, throughout the ages and today, have devoted themselves to the study and development of logic, far beyond the scope of this book. Here, however, it is enough—for my purposes in helping you to benefit from their wisdom for your objectives—to present the following ideas:

- The human mind is so constituted that the ability to reason is generally commensurate with an individual's intellectual capacity.
- If your prospect can respond to reasoning at all (the alternative being either demonstrational proof or an appeal to the emotions), he is capable of responding to your logic (even if he hasn't been trained or motivated to be logical in his own presentations).
- If you can read and understand most or all of this book, you are capable of being trained to be more logical than you may already be.
- Logic is the most efficacious way known, to reason effectively, arrive at facts and convey that reasoning to someone else.
- There is, essentially, only one kind of practical logic (for that purpose), and either you practice it just that way or you might as well not use it at all.
- Logic is the most effective way of finding out whether something (not demonstrable through the senses) is really a fact, and, once you know that it *is* a fact, of convincing someone else of this.
- That's the whole purpose of effective selling: To find out what the facts are regarding your prospect and convince him that they *are* facts (and are important to him).
- You can easily learn to be logical in your planning, thinking and communications.
    - —Here I'll introduce you to the basic principles.
    - —I'll give you many examples.
    - —Pretty soon you'll catch on to what it's all about.

—Your continued success in applying logic to your selling will come only with continued practice, self-evaluation and improvement.

—Before too long, you'll be able to use effective logic as easily as you can say or do anything you're now relying on for your selling efforts.

Logic and Questions

It's interesting—and significant—that the art of asking certain kinds of questions to make things happen, developed around the same time that logic did. This isn't surprising, since logic wanted to arrive at truth, and questions are a very important method of accomplishing this.

It is therefore safe to say that an important ingredient of effective logic is the wise use of questions. Incidentally, the effective knowledge and use of practical psychology also ties in with the value to successful selling of logic and questions. This is so for at least two reasons:

1. The rationale of logic and questions lies in the way in which the mind works.
2. The more you know about your prospect's psychology, the better you'll be able to select the questions to ask and the points to make.

Finally, remember what I've said before about the purpose of asking questions during your interview:

- First, you want to make sure that your objective for the call is proper and that you are on the right track.
- Second, once the answers to your questions reveal that you *are* on the right track, the continued use of the right kinds of questions (in the right sequence—dictated by logic, as we shall soon see) will get the prospect to tell *you* what you wanted to tell *him*.

HOW TO USE LOGIC AND QUESTIONS EFFECTIVELY

Now we're ready to accomplish *all* of the following goals:

—Explain how to use logic in a sales presentation.

—Show how this is most effectively done through the selected use of questions.

—Give examples of all principles as we develop them.

The best way I know of accomplishing the first two of the goals, stated just above, is to illustrate each concept with the details of *one* actual sales situation. Then I will develop a number of different, actual sales situations I've participated in and show how best to tackle them through logic and logical questions.

What logic is and how to use it	Example of each step, from an actual selling situation
1. Decide on your objective for the call, being armed with one (more, if advisable) alternative objective.	The salesman wants to make sure that the contractor-prospect can really benefit from the salesman's company's structural steel and accompanying services. If he can so benefit, the salesman wants the contractor to "buy" a survey of his needs.
2. Think through, and keep on experimenting with, statements/questions which will ultimately lead to the best "basic premise" (or *assumption*), as the beginning of your reasoning, which will combine *all* of these characteristics: a. The assumption is not too elementary, nor is it too close to the conclusion you want to arrive at (either to find the facts or convince the other of them). Only practice and experience will lead you to selecting the best premise. b. The assumption is definitely related to your objective. c. It is in itself a fact. (If you ask it as a question, then the answer must be a fact which leads you to either a continuation of your approach or an awareness that you're on the wrong track and should pursue another.) d. The premise must be fully accepted as a fact by the prospect.	How frequently do you use structural steel in your contracting work? (If he doesn't use it, or doesn't use it frequently enough to interest the salesman, or he doesn't do any contracting work at all, this will be revealed by the answer. If that's what turns out to be the situation, the salesman has achieved his first objective and must decide whether he wants to take up a different one or whether he ought to leave. If, however, the prospect answers with a figure, the salesman knows that the contractor does use structural steel and also whether the quantity is of interest to him. If it is, the question has established, in both of their minds, this basic premise: The prospect uses enough structural steel in his contracting work to make it worth the salesman's time to continue.)

What logic is and how to use it	Example of each step, from an actual selling situation
e. The premise is a natural and easy transition to the points the salesman wants to establish, and will inevitably lead to them.	
3. When your basic premise indicates that you are on the right track, think through the next statement you want made (by you or by him, the latter in response to a question you ask), having *all* of the following characteristics: a. It is a direct outgrowth and result of the previous statement (the basic premise). b. It is in itself true. c. It is directly related to, and should lead to, the ultimate conclusions you want to arrive at. d. The prospect accepts the fact that the statement is true.	What specifications do you require in the steel you use? (And, on the chance that he may not mention some that you know are important to him, which are among your product's strengths, you are ready to ask questions like: "How important to you is. . . ?", where you mention, one after another, those important specs which he has overlooked.) You have now further advanced your likelihood of succeeding because he is aware of his need for specs which, while he may not yet realize it, your product fills better than anyone else's, something he didn't know at first and couldn't readily learn through his senses. If *he* mentions the specs (even though you prompted him), he accepts their need as true.
4. Now you think of another statement which: a. Is a direct outgrowth of the relation between the preceding statement and your objective. b. Will further advance your objective. c. Is in itself true. d. Is accepted by the prospect as true.	Who lays out the quantities and kinds of steel you need for any one job?

What logic is and how to use it	Example of each step, from an actual selling situation
5. You do this progressively, with additional statements as needed (and revealed to you by his acceptance of the previous statements), all with the same characteristics as the one described above. (Only careful planning and experience will lead you to the correct statements and sequence, and questions are the best way to assure being always on the right track.)	a. What do you require of such men? (How important are the following qualities . . .?) b. What resources do you require for this layout? c. What other services do you require in this job? (How about . . . . ?) d. Who is now doing this for you? e. Are they meeting all of your requirements to your complete satisfaction? f. How much more does it cost you than you had expected because of this dissatisfaction?
6. When your judgment and experience have convinced you that he has accepted your facts, begin to show him that *you* can meet all of those requirements to his entire satisfaction, better than anyone else	I'm glad you have told me what you did, because everything you have expressed as a requirement is exactly what we are in a position to meet, to your complete satisfaction, better than anyone else.
7. Now begin to prove *each* of the claims you make.	Here, let me show you.

You said that you require:	Here's how we meet that requirement exactly, and better than anyone else.
(Now take up, one at a time, each requirement he mentioned.)	(For each one, provide your proof.)

What logic is and how to use it	Example of each step, from an actual selling situation
8. Use as your close the most natural outgrowth, which is, usually, "You said that you needed. . . . I've proven to you that we meet those needs exactly as you've stated them. Therefore there's no point in waiting any longer. I want the following kind of firm commitment from you *now*, in the form of. . . ." Of course, you won't use those words, you will be more subtle and polite—but make no mistake: I mean for you to be just as firm, decisive and insistent as my words imply.	Since I have shown you how my company provides you with exactly the kind of steel and services you need, better than your own people and anyone else in the market, when can our chief layout man come to see you to begin the work for you? He's available next Tuesday and Thursday. Which day do you prefer?
9. If you were mistaken in your belief that he was ready for the close, he'll raise objections. Handle them and move right in again with your close.	- - - -

FURTHER EXAMPLES

Now, for the rest of this chapter, I'm going to take each kind of sales-call objective and, present a case study (from my own experience) of how logic was applied successfully (using questions, where appropriate) in meeting that objective.

1. *OBJECTIVE:* To prospect with an existing customer.

    LOGICAL DEVELOPMENT: a. The customer is satisfied with your product or service. (What else can I do for you to make you completely satisfied with my product/ service?)

                      b. He should, as a professional businessman, want to help other, non-competitive businessmen to benefit from my product/service. (What non-competitors of yours would you like to help benefit from the same thing that has so satisfied you?)

    c. I'd like him to give me their names, addresses, etc.—including any information which will help me better sell them. (What information can you give me about them? How about their . . ?—specific information you want.)

    d. It may be helpful if I can use his name in approaching other prospect/non-competitors. (In calling on them, may I mention the fact that you recommended them to me?)

    e. I can keep his goodwill if I make him feel important because of his help. (How soon after I contact them would you like me to let you know how you've been able to help them?)

2. *OBJECTIVE*: To qualify a prospect.

    LOGICAL DEVELOPMENT: When you first approach a prospect, you want to find out certain things about him in order to decide whether to continue with him at all and/or what to talk to him about—and how best to do this. During a first interview, and in all subsequent visits, there may be many other details you'd like to know in order to determine whether and how best to proceed. All of this is called *qualifying* a prospect, and it must go on all the time, in every interview.

    The question technique in itself is, at the same time that it helps lead to a close in the right situations, a continuing qualifying process. Here, however, I want to talk about a sales call (or part of it) whose sole objective is to qualify (or further qualify) the prospect. I'll give you a list of the logical kinds of information you may want to have for the fulfillment of this objective, and logical questions to ask for each kind of qualifying.

    a. Does his company (or he) have a sufficient need for your product/service to make it worth your time to be with him? (How much . . . do you buy/use per . . . ?)

    b. Who is (are) the right person(s) to see. (Who makes the decisions on this matter?)

    c. Information necessary about the decision-maker(s) to facilitate calls. [When and where is the best time/place to see him (them)? How do I best go about seeing him (them)? What should I bring with me? What else can you tell me about his (their) interviewing, decision-making habits? What else should I know about him (them)?]

    d. The degree or extent to which my kind of product/service is being used. (From whom are you now getting this kind of product/service? Why from them? Why aren't you using it?)

    e. Where appropriate, the company's credit status. (What are your normal credit conditions for buying this kind of product/service?)

3. *OBJECTIVE:* To get to see the right person(s).

    LOGICAL DEVELOPMENT: This depends on whether you have to see only one person or more than one.

    a. Where you know that you have to see only one person, the logic is:

      (1) You must establish rapport with whomever serves as an intermediary between you and that person, in order to induce him to *want* to help you get to see the man you need. (It's so good of you to see me. How soon can you help me see Mr. Jones?)

      (2) You must resist the intermediary's efforts to prevent you from seeing the principal. (I appreciate your desire to help me. How much money is Mr. Jones losing per day by using his present filters? Well, that's why it's so important for me—or, as appropriate, you and me together—to see Mr. Jones real soon. How about now?)

      (3) If the principal is really not available at that time, you either wait a little while or make arrangements to come back when he *will* be available. (If I wait for him, how long will it be? Please give him my card with this note. I'll be back on . . . at . . . When can he see me. . . ? I'll phone him on. . . .)

    b. Where you know that you have to see more than one person, the logic is:

      (1) If you should see them all at the same time, or don't know whether you should, put that question or matter to the first qualified person you meet. (Would you prefer that I see all of the people individually or all at the same time?)

      (2) Now see whether he wants you to make the arrangements or whether he wants to make them for you. (Would you like me to contact them, or do you want to do it and let me know

when I'm to see them? I have these days and times open: . . . .)

(3) If it's appropriate (as in the case where you must first see the purchasing agent and get his approval for you to see another decision-making contributor), you want to make sure whether and/or when the first person you see (or any of the others) wants you to see him again. (After I see Mr. Smith, when may I come back to see you?)

4. *OBJECTIVE:* To find out the best objective for a call you are going to make because it is time to do so, where you either don't know or aren't sure of what's the best objective for that call.

LOGICAL DEVELOPMENT: a. You indicate that you are there that day because you are always interested in his business and you feel that this is a good time to renew the contact. (What can you tell me about developments affecting my company, since last I was here? Has anything come up since my previous visit to you?) If this is your first visit to him, and you don't know what your objective should be, you should tell him that you're there to see how you can be of service to him. (Since we've never met before, I thought I'd come to see you, get acquainted and find out how I can be of service to you. Which of my products/services are similar to what you are now using?)

b. Depending on his answers to your previous question(s), you ask additional questions until you find out whether it pays for you to continue that day (and for what), whether it would be better to arrange to come back some other time or decide that there's no point in coming back at all.

5. *OBJECTIVE:* To acquaint (or re-acquaint) the prospect with your company, your products/services and yourself, as a basis for some future call with an objective which would bring you closer to an eventual sale.

LOGICAL DEVELOPMENT: a. You want him to start thinking about your "package" so he'll be more receptive, at the right time, to a more significant objective. (How much do you know about my company and its products/services?)

b. You tell him what's most important about your

company, etc., in its most favorable light. (How did you react to the report in yesterday's newspapers about our new product. . . .?)

c. You make it plain that you are not trying to sell him now. (When you are ready to consider initiating the use of our product/service, what kind of information will you want?)

d. You want to leave him with something which will make for continuity. (To whom should I send this brochure when it comes out? When will be a good time to come and see you again?)

6. *OBJECTIVE:* To lay the groundwork necessary for your next call (s), where it isn't feasible to expect that one call is enough for getting an order.

LOGICAL DEVELOPMENT: a. You make it plain that you are talking about a particular product/service (line). (About how many units of . . . —your type of product/service—do you use per month?)

b. You want to get him thinking about the need for a change, at the right time, from what he is now using—to, preferably, *your* product/service. (When do you generally evaluate or re-evaluate whether your present items are the best available for you on the current market?

c. If he doesn't reply to this the way you'd like him to, you have to shake him out of his smugness by making him aware of something already on the market (don't identify it as yours unless he raises the point, and then, only incidentally) which is better for him than what he now uses. (What have you heard about the new. . . ?)

d. Once you can get him to indicate when he might be ready for the evaluation you want, you should try to find out how he's going to go about the evaluation. (When you do evaluate/re-evaluate your present items, what criteria do you use for your decisions?)

e. You now want to plant in his mind whichever of the following possibilities is adapted to your specific needs:

(1) When may I contact you to send one of our technical specialists to you for the evaluation?

(2) When can you come and see our unit in operation?

(3) How many samples of our unit would help you in that evaluation?

(4) When may I phone you, after the evaluation, for the next discussion between us?

(5) Which of the following specs (they happen to be mine, but I don't say so) are you going to look for in your evaluation?

7. *OBJECTIVE:* To get permission from the prospect to bid on one or more items he needs/will need, that you can supply.

LOGICAL DEVELOPMENT: a. You have to bring to the surface of his conscious mind that:

(1) He needs/will need items of the kind you provide very satisfactorily. (Which of these products/services of mine do you now/regularly/in the near future need?)

(2) He deals, for the supply of these items, only through bids. (What other method, besides bids, do you use for selecting suppliers?)

b. You want to make sure that even to bid, special approval is needed. (How does a supplier qualify to bid?)

c. You want to know the criteria for permission to bid. (What requirements must my company meet in order to get permission from you to bid?)

d. You must then show him how you meet those requirements to his complete satisfaction. (Will you evaluate our specifics . . . ? How do they stack up to your requirements?)

e. You must get him to commit himself firmly to allow you to bid. (What forms do you want us to fill out in bidding, and when must they be in your hands?)

8. *OBJECTIVE:* To get the prospect to let you help him write the specs for the bids he will solicit.

LOGICAL DEVELOPMENT: a. First you must establish clearly in his mind, and have expressed, the fact that he will be soliciting bids and that he hasn't yet written the bids. (How are you going to select your supplier? What specs are you using in judging the bids?)

b. Next you should get him to realize that the process of drawing up the specs is difficult, requires highly skilled specialists (whom he doesn't have) and would cost him more money to do himself than through spec-writing specialists. (What experience have you folks had in writing those kinds of specs? Did you find it easy or difficult? What kinds of specialists are needed for that task? How many such qualified specialists do you have? What is the comparative cost between writing them yourselves and having spec-writing specialists do it for you?)

c. Now you must take each one of the requirements for spec-writing (satisfactory to him), and show him, for each one, how your people meet them (as he, himself, stated them) better than anyone else, his own people included.

d. Then you must close by getting him to commit himself firmly to your proposal. (When can my chief spec-writer come in for the first tailoring session? He's free next Monday or next Wednesday. Which is better for you?)

9. *OBJECTIVE:* To find out the specs for a bid in which you are interested.

LOGICAL DEVELOPMENT: a. Get him to state that he is putting out for bids. (When are you inviting bids?)

b. Get him to indicate that you may bid. (What do we have to do to qualify to bid?)

c. Get him to tell you the specs—the close. (What are the specs on which we can make sure we're qualifying for your invitation to bid?)

10. *OBJECTIVE*: To get him to let you establish and prove the consumption by his prospects/customers of your products/services, which you want him to buy from you for re-sale to them.

LOGICAL DEVELOPMENT: a. Get him to admit that he will buy from you those quantities of those products/ services (offered by you) which will profitably be bought from him. (What criterion do you use in determining what products/services you buy for re-sale, and the quantities of those products/services? What relation do you see between that criterion and your suppliers?)

b. Get him to admit that he doesn't really know the extent to which your products/services sell or can sell most profitably (for him) to his prospects/customers. (What statistics do you now have to show you what products/services will sell most profitably?)

c. Ask him to let you provide him with valid statistics. (When may I come to see you with the kind of statistics you need? I can be ready in two weeks. Is the 15th better than the 16th?)

11. *OBJECTIVE*: Motivate dealers/distributors to move my products/services more profitably for me.

    LOGICAL DEVELOPMENT: a. They are now selling a certain volume of my products/services, but not to my satisfaction. (What volume are you now selling?)

b. The reason they aren't selling more is that they are not exerting their maximum/optimum efforts to saturate the market. (How come you aren't selling to the maximum market potential?)

c. They're falling short because they don't see enough in it for them. (What reasons other than profit could be motivating you to fall short in those efforts?)

d. They don't really know how much greater a profit there'd be for them if they sold more. (What statistics do you have on the margin of profit in my products/services compared to the competition? On the number of your customers who don't buy anything from you because they can't always get my product/service from you?)

e. Here are the statistics, so what are you waiting for? (In view of these statistics, when do you want the additional supply, Wednesday or Thursday?)

12. *OBJECTIVE*: Get the distributor/dealer to use some/more of my advertising/promotion ideas/materials.

    LOGICAL DEVELOPMENT: a. You know that you get a very satisfactory profit from selling my products/ services. (How does your profit from my products/services compare with the competition/other lines you carry?)

b. You aren't selling enough and therefore aren't getting maximum/optimum profit. (How much profit are you failing to get from not selling more of my lines?)

c. The chief reason you're not getting it is because you don't promote enough. (Why aren't you getting more people in for those sales?)

d. I have a program for you which will cost you nothing/little and get more customers in, not only for my lines but also for other lines you carry. (What do you think it would cost you to take my program?)

e. You'd better not wait any longer. (What time would be better for you to start the program, the last week of this month or the first week of next?)

13. *OBJECTIVE*: To get his approval for you to work with his salesmen.

LOGICAL DEVELOPMENT: a. Your salesmen aren't selling enough of my lines and others' (not competitive). (How well are your men doing in selling my lines? Other lines?)

b. The chief reason is that they don't know how. (Why?)

c. You don't have the time to train them. (How much time per week can you spare to train them?)

d. I can do a real good job on it without interfering with their other needs. (How much time can you allow me to train them?)

e. I'll keep you informed on my progress. (When may I start, and how soon after each visit do you want my report?)

14. *OBJECTIVE*: To arrange for him to visit my plant or another which has my line.

LOGICAL DEVELOPMENT: a. You won't be convinced of the great benefit to you of my product/service unless you see it in operation. (What else will it take to convince you that my product/service is the best you can get for your urgent need?)

b. Since I can't bring it here, you'll have to go elsewhere to see it in action. (When can you come with me to . . . to see it in action?)

15. *OBJECTIVE*: To get his approval for you to bring a specialist to see him.

LOGICAL DEVELOPMENT: a. I've gone as far as I can and must now bring in a specialist. (What do you still have to know before you say "yes"?)

b. How soon can I bring in our specialist to supply you with that information?

16. *OBJECTIVE*: To get his approval for a test.

LOGICAL DEVELOPMENT: a. The only thing that remains before you say "yes" is for you to see the results of a valid test. (What else do we have to do before you are finally convinced that my product/service is the best for exactly what you need?)

             b. I want to test it at my place or have you test it at your place. (How soon can we arrange for the necessary test and resulting report?)

17. *OBJECTIVE*: To make arrangements to tailor your product/service to his exact needs, at minimum cost.

    LOGICAL DEVELOPMENT: a. We both agree that it's best for you to have us tailor our program to your exact needs. (Do you want this package or do you want us to tailor one to your exact needs?)

             b. We don't want to spend more money on this than necessary to make the profit we must. (We have several different degrees of tailoring, depending on your budget for this. What's the top limit you're prepared to spend?)

             c. I'll have to come in real soon to begin the tailoring. (How soon can our specialist come in to begin the tailoring activity?)

18. *OBJECTIVE*: To get information from him on the progress of my bid or test.

    LOGICAL DEVELOPMENT: a. You have my bid/have begun a test. (When will you have finished considering my bid/running my test?)

             b. It's important for me to know the results because there may still be something I can do for your benefit. (What has been your experience with follow-ups by suppliers on bids/tests?)

             c. I'd like that information now so I can undertake whatever follow-up is good for you. (How soon can you let me know the results?)

19. *OBJECTIVE*: To get a firm commitment which represents the last step in the sale of that product/service to him.

    LOGICAL DEVELOPMENT: a. You've taken all the steps which had to precede this call. (Before we discuss the last step in our conversations, what else do you want me to tell you? Let me, first, review everything we agreed on in previous meetings. . . . Now, what remains?)

             b. The best way for me to provide this product/service to you is . . . (I can mail it to you or bring it. Which do you prefer? When, tomorrow or the next day?)

20. *OBJECTIVE*: To undertake the proper follow-up on a close already accomplished.

    LOGICAL DEVELOPMENT: a. You've already sold or promised him something and want to be sure he's satisfied with it. (What, if anything, still remains for me to do for your complete satisfaction with . . .?)

b. You want to know whether there's anything else he wants from you. (What else can I do for you?)

c. You want to try to get prompt entree for your next objective. (What will you need in the way of . . .? How soon? When will you be ready to see me in the next few weeks?)

21. *OBJECTIVE*: You want to keep in touch with him so he'll know you're always interested in him.

LOGICAL DEVELOPMENT: a. I have nothing to sell you now. (What do you need now from my lines?)

b. I want you to know that I'm always interested in you, even when I can't sell you anything. (How much time can you spare now just to chat? What can you tell me about your success in . . .?)

c. However, if there *is* anything I can do for you now I'm ready. (Is there anything I can do now to help you, and, if so, what?)

d. I want you to know now that I intend to come back again soon for the same reason. (What time of the week is best for you to have lunch with me?)

22. *OBJECTIVE*: To satisfy his complaint.

LOGICAL DEVELOPMENT: a. He has registered a complaint which I was sent to handle. (What are the exact details of your dissatisfaction?)

b. I can settle it to his complete satisfaction/have done so. (What would remain to be done, if anything, after I . . .?)

c. I don't want to go away until I know he's completely satisfied. (Is there any reason why you are still not completely satisfied, or can I tell my people that you're entirely pleased with what we've done to settle the matter?)

23. *OBJECTIVE*: To get him to recommend to you other people whom you might approach.

LOGICAL DEVELOPMENT: a. I am convinced that he is entirely satisfied with what I've done for him. (What else can I do to serve you to your complete satisfaction?)

b. I want him to realize that in recommending others to me, he's doing something good for himself.

(How would it interfere with your own strong position to recommend others to me?)

c. Therefore, I'd like him to give me some names and/or recommend them to me. (Who are the people you think would appreciate your recommendation? What details can you give me about them, like: . . .? Which of them can you contact yourself to tell them about me?)

Summary

1. You must prove to your prospect that what you say is *truly* of great benefit to him.
2. If you can do so through one or more of the five senses, that is the best way.
3. If, however, the senses can't help you, you must prove to him the facts of your presentation through the proper use of logic.
4. To do so you must:

   a. Start with a proper basic premise which is in itself true, is important to your thinking and communication of the fact and is accepted as true by him.

   b. Develop a series of statements, one growing out of the other, each of which is true, is accepted by him as true and advances your process of convincing him.

5. The best way to do this is by converting each of these statements into one or more questions which will get *him* to say what *you* wanted to tell him.

CHAPTER **7**

How to Use
Semantics in the Magic
Sales Question Technique

In all face-to-face selling interviews, you must say certain things to the prospect and he will say certain things to you. In addition to all the gestures and physical demonstrations that will be employed, the bulk of the communication will be through words.

While everything I intend to say in this chapter has some or much practical applicability to the *written* word, here I shall concentrate on the *spoken* word.

Since many of the words you use in your selling situation have many possible correct, different meanings, here's what might happen:

- You use one or more words with *your* meaning for them in *your* mind, and the prospect, on hearing them interprets them *his* way—different from yours.
- He uses one or more words with *his* meaning for them in *his* mind, and you, on hearing them, interpret them *your* way—different from his.

Result? Poor or ineffective communication, leading to weaker explanations, proof and conviction. Nobody makes anything happen.

Definition

Semantics is the study and art of using words correctly and accurately between two (or among more than two) people, so that each one understands every word in exactly the same way as its user intended it.

Here I shall be telling you how to use semantics to increase and improve your selling communication.

HOW TO BECOME A MAKE-HAPPEN SEMANTICIST

If you want to increase your selling ability, here are some tips:

A. Read any elementary book on semantics recommended to you by your local librarian. You'll find it extremely interesting, and it will open your eyes to a whole new world of effective selling communication. If you wish, you can do more advanced reading or studying after that, but it won't be necessary for your purposes.

B. Become aware of the *fact* that many words you want to use, or that you hear, can have different meanings in your mind from the ones in the prospect's mind. Therefore, don't be so ready to use any old word without first checking on whether your *key* selling words fall into this semantic problem. And don't be so quick to assume that your prospect is using *his* key words in exactly the way you're interpreting them.

C. Review the key words in your presentation, look them up in a good dictionary and remember which ones require semantic clarification.

D. When you talk to your prospect, try to avoid using those words which lend themselves to more than one meaning, and use one, if possible, which is *not* capable of such confusion. If, however, you *must* use such multi-meaning words, surround each word with other words in such a way that your meaning is clear.

E. When your prospect talks to you, make sure to check whether he really means what you *think* he does.

But, by far, the best way to engage in effective semantics is through the use of questions, and that's what we're going to take up now.

MAGIC QUESTIONS AS AN ASSURANCE OF SEMANTIC ACCURACY

While there are a number of different ways to make sure that you and the prospect are using the same word in the same way, nothing is as effective as the proper use of questions for that purpose.

Here's how it works:

You Are Talking

Suppose you want to make things happen and get a point across to your prospect, like:

> "The reason you should buy my *Extra Expense Insurance Policy* is that it makes it possible for you to continue to run your business with no extra capital in case of fire in your plant."

I heard the salesman in this case say:

> "With my policy, you will have enough coverage to continue to run your business at no extra expense to you, in the event of a fire loss."

Let's analyze some of the weaknesses of interpretation which might result, in the prospect's mind, from hearing that statement.

- *Coverage* is a technical insurance term which is vague to an inexperienced prospect, although perfectly clear to the salesman. There are all kinds of coverage.
- *Extra expense* can mean several different things: *additional* expense; *unneeded* expense; *unexpected* expense; extra *cost*; extra *outlay*; etc.
- *Run your business in the event of a fire loss*: What effect does the fire have on the business? How does the coverage aid in running the business? Etc.

Now, all of the ideas expressed by that salesman were true and applicable to the situation, but they were not clear to the prospect. Since the salesman *had* to express those thoughts, he could have clarified his meaning by asking the following questions (and known, by the answers, whether the prospect really understood the situation):

1. What effect would a fire in your plant have on your ability to continue to run your business?
2. As you are presently set up, if you had to repair or re-build your plant after a fire, where would you get the money?
3. If you couldn't get the money right away, what effect would this have on your profit while the burned-down plant was not repaired or re-built?
4. How does this loss of profit compare to the cost of the premium on my *Extra Expense Insurance Policy?*

He Is Talking

Now suppose your prospect is saying something, either in response to something you have said or on his own initiative. For example:

"The reason I want to give some of my business to your competitor is that in that way better service is guaranteed."

I heard a prospect actually say that to the salesman I was out with on a call. The salesman immediately started to argue that two suppliers did *not* represent better service.

It's like the patron of a restaurant who tasted the food the waiter had brought him and said that it wasn't fit for pigs; whereupon, the waiter tried to convince him that it was.

Where Did the Salesman Fall Down?

He didn't recognize the semantic vagueness of the prospect's statement. He unconsciously interpreted it his own way, if he really listened fully at all, and barged right in to contest *his own* interpretation of what the prospect had said.

As a good semanticist, he would have reasoned as follows:

a. What the prospect said is capable of a number of different meanings.
b. What did he mean by *better service* and *guarantee?*

c. I'd better ask him just what he meant by his key words and respond to his *real* meaning.

And the best way he could have done this was to ask the right kinds of questions. What he should have said was:

1. I'm not entirely sure I know exactly what you mean, so I'd like to ask you some questions.
2. How do you get better service by giving some of your business to my competitor? Better service than what? Better service than I give you?
3. What do you mean by the word *guarantee?* Does he guarantee better service *in writing* than we do? What kinds of assurance of service do you want? We can check to see whether we aren't already giving it to you, and, if not, what we have to do to give it to you.

EXAMPLES OF KEY WORDS REQUIRING SEMANTIC CARE

1. TERM: *Create a need.*

   PROBLEM: Many salesmen are taught, or read somewhere, that they must *create* a need (desire, interest, etc.) in the prospect's mind/emotion for the salesman's product/service.

   SOLUTION: a. To *create* means to *originate.*
   b. Effective selling requires that the prospect *have* a need (desire, interest, etc.) which the product/service can properly meet.
   c. If the word *create* is used with semantic looseness, the salesman believes that he must create the *need* rather than an *awareness* (on the part of the prospect) of a need (etc.) which already exists.
   d. To create a need, in the true sense of the word, is to originate one which may not really be a true one.
   e. Good selling requires that the salesman find out what the prospect needs or desires and create an awareness in the prospect that his need or desire is best met by your product/service.
   f. This is what is really intended by the false use of the term; it is, therefore, better not to use or think of that expression at all.
   g. The salesman should constantly be guided by the requirement to create an *awareness* of a need.

2. TERM: *Cheaper.*

   PROBLEM: The word *cheap* always conveys a sense of less worthiness.

   SOLUTION: Never use that word to describe your product or service. Use: *less expensive, more economical, less costly, lower-priced.*

3. TERM: *Competitive.*

PROBLEM: The word can mean:
  a. In general, pertaining to or characterized by competition.
  b. As many salesmen use it, just as good (economical, etc.) as that of the competition.

SOLUTION: Don't use the word at all. Say: just as good quality; equal in price; etc.

4. TERM: *Quality*.

PROBLEM: The word, which frequently *must* be used, is vague; it doesn't convey the *extent* of the quality, which is the most important aspect of the term.

SOLUTION: Say: *high* quality; *superior* quality; the quality called for in the specs; etc. The best way to handle the problem is to ask the question: "What level of quality are you looking for?" (Preferably, add some specific criterion as a guide to his answer.) Then tell and show him how your product meets that requirement better than any other product/service in that line.

5. TERM: *Prompt delivery*.

PROBLEM: The word *prompt* can mean:
  a. In the dictionary: performed *at once, at the moment, on the spot;* immediate; right away.
  b. In the salesman's mind: as soon as our men go out; as soon as we process the order; every Tuesday; etc.
  c. In the prospect's mind: at the very moment I need or want it; today; tomorrow; etc.

SOLUTION: Avoid the word and be more pinpointed: by 3 p.m. next Tuesday; not later than 5 p.m. today; etc. If you don't know what he expects in satisfactory delivery time, ask him: "How long can you give me to have it in your hands; will three days be all right?"

6. TERM: *To your satisfaction*.

PROBLEM: The term is too vague. What will satisfy him may not be what *you* think will satisfy him.

SOLUTION: Avoid the word. Ask him: "What requirements have you set for your use of the product/service?" (Spell out the criteria if you can: time of delivery; durability; lead time after order; tolerances; etc.)

7. TERM: *Acceptance*.

PROBLEM: Many salesmen use this word in an expression like: "My product/service has very wide *acceptance*." This word is vague and almost a cliché. It doesn't mean *enthusiastic* use or, necessarily, more than average favor. It doesn't, therefore, particularly impress the prospect.

SOLUTION: Don't use the word. Say something like: My product/service is used by ... thousand companies with complete enthusiasm; practically everybody in your trade area clamors for it; everyone knows about it and wants it.

8. TERM: *Customer-oriented.*

PROBLEM: I have heard salesmen say: "My company is 'customer oriented'." This is an empty, relatively meaningless expression. What company (sending out a salesman) isn't interested in selling to the prospect? *Oriented* means different things to different people and doesn't necessarily convey what you really want to say. The word itself means, according to the dictionary: placed to face the east; adjusted to defined relations; put in the right position; knowing one's bearings.

SOLUTION: Don't use the term. Say something like: my company is more interested in the prospect's (customer's) welfare than our competitors; we're always at your call; we do everything we can to meet your needs; etc.

9. TERM: *Reliable.*

PROBLEM: The salesman says that he, his company and/or his product/ service are *reliable*. This is a relative term. The prospect may wonder: *How* reliable? Reliable for what? More reliable than the competition?

SOLUTION: Ask the prospect what he requires in follow-through by you, your company and/or your product/service. For example:
  a. What do you require in number of days between placing the order and receiving it?
  b. How frequently do you want me to call on you?
  c. What arrangements do you expect for free repairs?
  d. How long do you expect the item to last?

Then tell and show him how you, your company and/or your product/service meet those requirements or wishes fully, even more than he has stated it and/or better than your competition.

10. TERM: *More complete line.*

PROBLEM: When a salesman says "We have a more complete line," he can have the following effect on the prospect:
  a. If a line is *complete,* how can anything be *more* complete? *Complete* is an absolute term not permitting comparison. The word, therefore, can strike him as being meaningless.
  b. There isn't a sufficiently specific comparison by product/ service between your line and that of the competition, related to the *prospect's* needs.

SOLUTION: Say something like: our line is complete for all of your needs, which nobody else can truthfully say; we have a product/service for every one of your needs; if you deal with us, you won't have to go to anyone else to get exactly what you need, when you need it, in the way you need it.

11. TERM: *Limited distribution.*

PROBLEM: The salesman wants to convey to the dealer/distributor the idea that if he takes on this line, he'll have no competition (or limited competition) from other dealers/distributors (in his trade area) for the same product or something similar, and that, therefore, he will make a greater profit from carrying this line. The term *limited distribution,* however, is vague and can mean different things to each of them. *How* limited? What does *distribution* mean? Distribution to *whom, when, where?*

SOLUTION: First ask the prospect some questions.

a. How close is your nearest competitor?

b. In what lines does he compete with you?

c. How much of a profit could you make from my line if he didn't carry it or anything as good as it?

Then you can tell and show him that:

• You will not (do not) sell your line to that competitor.

• The competitor cannot carry any competitive or better products/services in that line.

• People wanting anything anywhere near what your line supplies will *have* to go to him.

• His profits will, therefore, be much greater than they now are if he will consistently carry your line.

12. TERM: *Support.*

PROBLEM: Salesmen selling to dealers/distributors, wanting to establish that they will help the latter's own salesmen effectively sell the products/services in question, have been heard to say: "We will give *full support* to your salesmen." This is a vague term and can mean something entirely different to the prospect from what you have in mind.

SOLUTION: Ask him questions like the ones indicated here:

a. How important is it to you to have your men sell high volumes of this kind of product/service?

b. How well-equipped are they now in the ability to sell it effectively?

c. How much time can you personally spare to improve their ability to sell it effectively?

d. How many days a month can you spare them to work with me?

e. What arrangements can we make now so I can help them on those days?

13. TERM: *Availability.*

PROBLEM: I have heard many salesmen say something like: "My product/service has greater availability." The word is a relative one and also is vague, because there are different levels involved.

SOLUTION: Ask him:

a. How frequently will you require additional shipments (supplies, people) from us?

b. How much lead time will you require between the communication of your need and the time you have it filled?

c. How many will you require at any one time?

Then tell and show him how you are fully equipped to meet every one of his needs, exactly and fully, as he has stated them.

14. TERM: *Same* or *similar.*

PROBLEM: The prospect says something like: "I've already tried something similar to (like) your product/service, and it doesn't work." or, "I already have the same thing (something similar, just like it)."

SOLUTION: Ask him to pinpoint the sameness or similarity, somewhat like this:

a. Does your product/service have these qualities exactly, or do they differ: . . . .?

b. What degree of difference is there?

c. How important to you is that degree of difference?

Then you can point out to him that what you are offering is really not the same as, or similar to, what he now has or has tried, but superior—and *exactly* suited to his needs, which the other is/was not.

AN EXPERIENCE

I want to interrupt the listing of semantic problems/solutions to tell you of a situation in which I found myself. It illustrates the importance of pinning people down to the exact meanings of the words they use, and having confidence in your "package" and the courage to promote your line.

Several years ago, a company invited me to come and see their entire top management team to explain how I could help them re-organize their sales force to make sales happen faster. When I had finished asking my questions and showing how I would meet their needs exactly, better than anyone else, the Chief Executive Officer said: "I agree with you, Bill, that we have to re-organize our sales the way you say. But we can do this without your help, by ourselves."

I immediately replied, "You want to bet?"

Now, what did I have in mind? Simply that he didn't want to commit himself to engaging my services, or he didn't want to take the trouble to make the changes he realized were necessary, because it was so comfortable to go along as he was.

I got the assignment at once. Several years later, the Chief Executive Officer told me that that one question of mine ("You want to bet?") tipped the scales in my favor, because it helped him face the facts of his attempt to procrastinate and his unwillingness to make changes. Besides, he felt that my confidence and daring in making that statement represented the kind of service he needed and wanted.

BACK TO OUR EXAMPLES

Now let's continue with terms used by salesmen which lead to semantic confusion or weakness.

15. TERM: *Above average.*

PROBLEM: A salesman wants to convey to the prospect that the salesman's product/service will yield a markup to the prospect higher than anything he can get from a product/service in that range of items to be sold. He uses the term *above average* to express that thought.

The difficulty here is that:

a. *Average* is a word that means different things to different people.

b. Its strict meaning is the total number of units (dollars, etc.) divided by the total number of items. For example: If you sell ten items, all at different prices ($5 for one, $10 for another, etc.), the total sales volume could be $275. The *average* price or return could then be stated as $27.50. So what!

c. Just how much *above* average (whatever that means) would be of interest to the prospect?

SOLUTION: Don't use the word *average* at all. Ask questions like these:

a. What's the minimum markup you can have on this line and still want to carry it?

b. What markup are you now getting on the line you're now carrying?

c. What markup would you consider possible and desirable?

Then tell and show him how:

- Your product/service consistently exceeds the minimum markup he is accustomed to getting and accepting.
- By carrying your markup, he comes closer to (or further than) the goal he has set for himself, in comparison to any other line.

16. TERM: *Profit.*

PROBLEM: The salesman wants to convince the prospect that the product/service being offered is of greater financial benefit to the prospect than that of the competition (or than not carrying anything like it at all). The salesman uses the word *profitable* or *profit* to describe what will result from the purchase.

The word *profit* (profitable) may not be the correct one, and if it isn't, the prospect won't be convinced.

Profit for a company represents the difference between its total sales volume (plus any other sources of income it may have) and the total costs for the entire company (including the price paid for your product/service). The *only* person who *can* show a profit for an entire company is its Chief Executive Officer. Therefore, if you talk *profit* to anyone but him, you aren't really saying anything that is meaningful to *him*. He knows (consciously or unconsciously) that he can't control company *profit* and is therefore not impressed with your argument.

SOLUTION: Unless you're talking to the Chief Executive Officer (or, if you're talking to him, unless your product/service in itself represents a profit—where you can show that the total cost/price of what you have to offer yields a residue from its sale representing absolute company-wide profit), use the word *profitability* or *contribution* to profit. The most effective way to accomplish your purpose is to ask questions like these:

a. What contribution to profit do you hope to make by selling my product/service to your customers (by using my raw materials)?

b. What role does the cost of my product/service (and/or its durability) play in that profitability?

c. What do you expect to charge your customers for the finished product/service?

Then produce your figures to show how:

- The cost of buying/using your product/service is as low as it can be for his needs.

- The price he can get from your product/service is as high as he can get from anything, if not higher.
- This makes for a greater contribution by him to company profit than what your competition has to offer or than his not buying your (kind of) product/service at all.

17. TERM: *Afford.*

    PROBLEM: The prospect says that he can't *afford* to buy your product/ service now, or at all. He may not mean what you *think* he does by that word. If you don't challenge his meaning, you may either become unjustifiably discouraged or too insistent, depending on what he *does* mean.

    SOLUTION: Ask him what he means by the word *afford.* Here's a suggested wording:

      a. You say you can't *afford* to buy it. Do you mean that you have no budget for it? (If so, when will your budget allow for it?)

      b. Do you mean that it's too costly for your ability to contribute properly to profit? (If so, let's see whether that's really so.)

ANOTHER EXPERIENCE

Very often a prospective client of mine will interview me for the possibility of my running a training program for his salesmen. He agrees (and is fully convinced) that: his salesmen are inadequately trained; he is not satisfied with their results; he has no one inside his company who can adequately train them; he likes my approach and ability; he doesn't want anyone of lesser caliber.

Then, when he hears what it will cost him to engage me for the program, he says: "I can't afford your services."

My questions and statements to him generally run something like this:

- Do you mean you don't have the budget (and can't get one) or that you don't want to spend that much money from budget?
- If the latter is his case: How much do you suppose it's costing you in less profitable sales (volume mix or cost of sales) because your men are inadequately trained?

I then wind up by saying, "Your situation isn't that you can't afford to undertake and follow through on this kind of training. The fact is, you can't afford *not* to start on the training—and right away."

A FEW MORE SEMANTIC PROBLEMS

Now let's wind up this chapter with some more examples of loose or undesirable semantics.

18. TERM: *Closer.*

PROBLEM: The prospect says that my competitor's facility (for making available to him the product or service I'm offering) is *closer* to his plant (office, etc.) than mine. Since the word *closer* is a comparative, we need something valid to compare it with. Is mere physical proximity the only thing he has in mind? And if he does, is he justified in that conviction?

SOLUTION: Again, questions come to the rescue. Just ask him:

a. How long does it take between the time that you ask them for something and the time you get it?

b. How much more important is this to you than the superior benefits to you (already agreed on) of my product/service.

Then tell and show him (as applicable) that:

- While you are a little farther away, you can get it to him just as fast (if not more so).
- The slight time edge that the competition has is not as important to him as the greater benefit of your product/service.

19. TERM: *Exclusive territory.*

PROBLEM: A dealer/distributor wants an "exclusive" if he is to take on your line. The word can mean something different to him from what it does to you.

SOLUTION: Pinpoint the conditions of what *you* mean by *exclusive,* along as many of the following lines as apply to you:

a. No other dealer/distributor in a clearly stated area will be allowed to carry the line (with any specific exceptions you want to make).

b. He *must* meet certain minimum quotas of sales if he is to enjoy the privilege, these quotas being spelled out clearly.

c. He *must* meet specifically stated conditions and terms.

d. He *must* sign *your* contract.

20. TERM: *Durable.*

PROBLEM: The word in itself means only that it will last, without saying how long. This can create either:

a. A different meaning in his mind from yours; or

       b. A feeling of vagueness in his mind, which will make him discount the importance to him of your statement.

SOLUTION: If you must use the word, surround it with other words which will indicate clearly and precisely how long you claim the item will last. Another approach is to state exactly how long it will last under clearly defined conditions. An additional piece of advice is this: Before you start telling him how long your product/service will last, ask him how important that quality is to him.

21. TERM: *In stock.*

PROBLEM: Often the crucial point which determines whether a prospect will order from you *now* is how much of your (kind of) material he now has in the kind of situation which meets his needs, both present and future (near and distant). The expression *in stock* can be vague and/or misleading because it means different things to different people.

SOLUTION: Ask him questions which will reveal both his needs and his true situation, like:

       a. How much of this material do you need to be able to put your hands on whenever you need it?

       b. How much of this material do you now have physically present in your warehouse, ready to be used at a moment's notice?

       c. How much of it is in the supplier's warehouse, ear-marked for you? How long would it take you to get it after you indicated that you wanted it at once?

       d. How much of it is on order with a supplier but not yet filled? How long would it take to get it?

22. TERM: *Expertise.*

PROBLEM: Many salesmen talk to their prospects about their company's *expertise* as a benefit to the prospect. The trouble with that word is:

       a. It's vague and doesn't indicate *how much* "expertise" is involved.

       b. It might bother certain people as a word because it seems unjustifiably boastful.

SOLUTION: Don't use the word at all. Find out how much specialized, technical skill they need and prove that you have it.

23. TERM: *Loyalty.*

PROBLEM: Your prospect says he agrees that what you have to offer is of benefit to him, but he's already buying from a long-time supplier who has been good to him. He feels a sense of *loyalty* to that supplier and doesn't want to hurt him in any way.

SOLUTION: Get him to break the word *loyalty* down to its barest elements and attack *those*, without upsetting his concept of loyalty. The right kinds of questions will accomplish this; for example:

a. How well does he meet your specs, as you described them to me?

b. In what respects does he meet them as well as I do?

c. What benefits do you fail to get from him that you can get from me?

d. Which is more important to you, not hurting his feelings or getting the best product/service for your company?

24. TERM: *Committed.*

PROBLEM: You want the prospect to buy something from you which he agrees meets his requirements exceedingly well, but he says he's already *committed* to someone in your competition. If you let him get away with just that word, you may not be understanding accurately exactly what he means, since different people use the word differently.

SOLUTION: Ask him questions to pinpoint the kind of commitment he has in mind, and then attack what he really means. For example: Is your contract with him in writing or have you simply discussed the terms with him? What kind of obligation do you have to him, moral or legal? What has he already done that represents an expense to him for that commitment? How far have *you* gone to implement the commitment?

25. TERM: *Problems.*

PROBLEM: The prospect says that he has heard of other customers of yours who've had *problems* with your product/service. If you don't get him to specify the exact (kinds of) problems, he'll continue to be convinced that they exist, are insurmountable and good reason for not buying from you. The trouble is that the word *problem* means different things to different people.

SOLUTION: Ask him questions like:

a. What kind(s) of problems?

b. Who had it (them)?

c. Why did he think he had a problem?

d. Did he report it to our man on his frequent visits there?

e. What do you know about how the so-called problem was solved?

26. TERM: *Get approval.*

PROBLEM: The man you're talking to says he likes what you have to offer. If it were up to him, he'd buy it right away. But, says he, he has to *get approval* from. . . . He may not really mean what you think he does. He may really be saying he wants a confirming opinion, or the opportunity for someone else to feel he's part of the decision.

SOLUTION: Ask him who he has to consult, and exactly why, so you can give him any additional information or help he may need in order to convey to the other person the exact message you gave to him. Ask him whether you may accompany him when he consults the other person, in case any questions arise not already touched on. Don't hesitate to ask him who makes the final decision. If it's he, try to get him to give you a firm commitment *now*, so you can start implementing it at once (for his benefit), even though no one in his company need know about it until he's talked with the other person.

27. TERM: *Production.*

PROBLEM: The prospect says that he's getting all the *production* he wants out of his present machine and doesn't, therefore, need yours. You know that yours has the advantage, that it costs less to operate *your* machine for the same production. You now have to make him see the difference between the two concepts.

SOLUTION: Tell him that you want to distinguish between *production* and *productivity.* To do this, ask him:

a. What does he mean by *production* (total machine output)?

b. How important to him is *productivity* (output by the machine by man-hour and other costs)?

Then show him how your machine not only has the same *production* as his present machine but also has better *productivity.*

Summary

1. A word important to your sales communication can have more than *one* correct meaning.
2. If you use or hear a word with one meaning in mind, and the prospect has another meaning in mind, there is ineffective communication.
3. The study and practice of the art of using and interpreting words exactly as they are intended to be used is called *semantics*.
4. Semantics is very important to you as a salesman.
5. To practice it you must:
   a. Be constantly alert to the words used in a sales call and ask yourself which ones are capable of more than one meaning.
   b. Wherever possible don't use such words yourself, but if you must, surround them with other words which will make your meaning perfectly clear to the prospect.
   c. When the prospect uses a word whose meaning could be different in his mind from the way you interpret it, don't respond to it until you really understand exactly what he had in mind.
6. The most effective way to make sure that your semantics work properly for you is to ask questions:
   a. Before he uses a confusing word, because you can then prevent it by the nature of the words your question employs.
   b. By asking him what he means, exactly, when he uses a confusing word.

CHAPTER **8**

How to Make
Things Happen on
Actual Calls with the
Magic Question Technique

Now, before I finish up the book with the role of questions in handling objections, I'm ready to take everything I've said so far and tie it **all** together. In this chapter, I shall show how the steps described in previous chapters can be brought to the happy ending we all want.

<h2 style="text-align:center">REVIEW OF THE MAGIC</h2>

Let's first re-state the concept of selling revolving around the question-asking technique.

1. The ultimate goal of all sales calls is for you, the salesman, to come away with a firm order from the prospect to buy something from you, directly or indirectly, according to what you offer him.

2. In some kinds of businesses, it is both possible and desirable to make the objective of *each* call the acquisition of such a firm order. In other kinds of businesses, and/or for certain types of prospects/situations, this objective is either never feasible or only sometimes attainable. In that kind of setup, there must be *two* objectives:

   a. The long-range objective still remains the same—to get a firm order.

   b. The immediate objective for one specific call can be any one or more of many, which have already been listed. Of course, if the prospect is ready to *give* you the order, no matter what the objective was for *that* call, by all means take it.

3. So—while you must never depart from your long-range objective, you should build your entire approach around *each* call, relating it to all the other calls on the same prospect.

4. *Maximizing your chances for success.*

   You have only so many hours in any one week to make things happen. The greater number of such hours that you spend in calling on qualified prospects—who will go along with your valid objectives for your calls on them—the greater your chances for overall success for your company and you.

Conversely, any time you spend with a prospect who will *not* go along with your valid objectives for calling on him, or whose benefit to your company or you is less than you would derive from another prospect, is reducing your overall chances for success.

Therefore, since you want to be as successful as possible, you must so plan your work and implement your plans that you waste as little time as possible (when prospects *can* be seen), either by not calling on prospects at all or wasting time between calls (where those time lags are avoidable), or by spending more time with a prospect than is really necessary.

5. *Assuring success before any one call.*

Even before you plan a call on a prospect, you must begin to carry on constant effort to maximize your call time. This requires that you *always:*

- a. Make sure that you really *want* to be a salesman (and a successful one).
- b. Make sure that you really believe in (and want to work for) your company, no matter what its shortcomings may be.
- c. Learn everything you can about your company and the products/ services you have to sell.
- d. Make sure always to have the most current and extensive list of prospects in your territory.
- e. Learn as much as you can about each prospect, so you can:
  - (1) Decide whether to call on him at all.
  - (2) Know how frequently to call on any one prospect, and with what intervals.
  - (3) Be mindful of the best priorities of calls among prospects.
- f. Know your competition thoroughly.

6. *Be enthusiastically convinced that the "package" you represent*—your company, your product(s)/service(s)—*is the very best for any one prospect on whom you call.*

7. *Plan your time carefully.*

- a. Plan your call cycles in such a way that you spend as little time as possible going from one prospect's location to another's, or waiting for a prospect to see you.
- b. Have everything you'll need for the trip ready in advance, and in good, available condition.
- c. Plan to get an early start. (And don't neglect any opportunity during the day to be with a *qualified* prospect.)

8. *Plan each call effectively.*

- a. Select your prospects wisely, so you're calling on those most important to your company and you, in the best possible priorities.

b. Be sure that you have, for each prospect so selected, the most likely objective for that call, with alternative objectives where advisable or necessary.

c. Use a planning sheet like the one I suggested in a previous chapter, listing your first thoughts about what you might say during the interview.

d. On that same sheet, re-arrange those thoughts in the most logical/chronological sequence possible.

e. Convert each such statement into a question, the answer to which should lead to that statement.

9. *When you are finally admitted to see the person you want to interview:*

a. Greet him and let him know/review for him who you are, your company and *the fact that you are a salesman* (proud to be one).

b. Thank him for seeing you.

c. Establish/re-establish and maintain rapport with him.

d. Capture his undivided attention and keep it all through the interview, pausing when it is distracted and picking it up again.

BEGINNING TO CLOSE

Now let's re-state the concept of the close that I've been developing all along and relate it to the ability of this "magic formula of the question," to help you make the close happen more often.

A. You have an objective for that call. If, during the interview, you discover that the objective you've selected is not the best, or is infeasible altogether, you must be prepared to switch to another better one and pursue that one.

B. You want to achieve that objective completely before you leave him that day. In order to accomplish this, you will have to do and say certain things. At some point or other, you'll have to say or do something to get him to commit himself firmly to do or say what you wanted him to. That statement or action by you is what I call *initiating* the close; *his* statement or action (representing his firm commitment) is the *close* itself—the achievement of your objective.

C. If, when you initiate (or re-initiate after you've fielded his objections), you can't get a close satisfactory to you, that must mean that you *failed* in that interview (and wasted your time) for any one or more of the following reasons:

1. You omitted one or more of the steps and criteria I outlined above in the Review of the Magic.

2. You didn't perform one or more of those steps properly.

3. You took the steps in an improper sequence.

4. You had the wrong objective for that call.

5. You hadn't qualified the prospect properly.

6. This was the wrong time or place to interview him.

7. You didn't plan well or accurately enough.

8. You didn't ask your questions properly and/or respond properly to his answers.

9. You didn't prove effectively the statements you made.

10. You didn't initiate the close properly or at the right time.

11. You didn't handle his objections properly.

12. You didn't re-initiate the close promptly or properly.

ALERTNESS TO SIGNALS

The most important aspect of maximizing interview time is to be alert throughout the entire interview to signals which the prospect may be sending out (consciously or unconsciously) that he is:

- Not receptive to you or what you are saying.
- Not interested.
- Not ready for you.
- Doesn't understand.
- Isn't convinced.
- Is hostile to you.
- Wants you out of there.

If he sends such a signal, at any time, you must recognize it at once and either:

—Do or say what's necessary to overcome the cause of the signal; or

—Realize that there's no point in staying there any more that day, and (leaving the door open for another visit, if desirable, under more favorable circumstances) bow out gracefully and quickly. This makes it possible for you to spend the remaining time (that you had planned to spend with *him*) to see an additional, more receptive prospect, whom you hadn't thought you'd have time to see that day.

QUESTIONS AS SIGNAL-ALERTERS AND CLOSE-EXPEDITERS

Here's where the question technique serves a dual purpose:

1. It keeps you constantly alert to signals, because you keep on asking questions in the proper sequence and analyze his answers. These will clearly indicate to you whether:

    a. You're on the right track, in which case you continue as planned.

    b. You should change your objective and pursue *it*.

    c. You should get out of there quickly and ply your wares in a better
       marketplace.
2. If your questions reveal that you are on the right track, they are
   simultaneously advancing your cause and leading directly and firmly to the
   close.

MAKE-HAPPEN QUESTIONS AND THE CLOSE

Even though you must, at the proper moment, *initiate* the close, the magic formula of the question is, in a sense, a continuing initiation *and* culmination of the close. Let me show you what I mean.

- Each question *pushes* the prospect's thinking farther along the logical and chronological path, where he becomes more and more aware of a need or desire he has which (while he doesn't yet realize it) can be satisfied *only* by what you have to offer.
- When he's finally drooling for something which will satisfy that need or desire, you show him how what you're offering does it precisely, and better than anything else.
- He's now completely ready to commit himself firmly to what you are offering, but you still have to nudge him to say or do something to externalize and concretize that readiness.

Thus, through this technique, you *begin* to initiate the close (and I recognize the redundancy of those words, but it's what I mean) with the first question, and (unless the anti-continuation signals require a cessation or re-alignment of the troops) you continue the closing attack until it's time to finalize the close (another purposeful repetitiveness) by saying or doing what's necessary to get *him* to say or do what makes his commitment firm.

The whole point is that the *closing* process should be a continuing, properly developing one, leading to the *final* close effort at the right time and in the right way.

And, if the closing attack is interrupted by objections (at any point), you handle them and immediately *resume* the closing efforts.

Now let's list the actual steps of the question-close technique.

1. You've captured his attention, which means that all the steps which precede that one (as I described them above) have been satisfactorily taken.
2. You now say something like this: "Mr. Jones, I don't want to waste either your time or mine. I want to talk to you only if what I have to offer you today is exactly what you need or want. In order to know that, I have to ask you some questions, so here goes."

3. You then begin to ask your questions, as planned the night before, with these cautions:

    a. You'd better remember what you planned the night before, but if you have to refer to your notes, do so as unobtrusively as possible; don't let him see them and don't allow too much silence to elapse.

    b. Ask the questions even if you know the answers, and as though you didn't.

    c. Remember that your questions must be calculated to make him aware of a need or desire for the *kind* of offer you're prepared to make (so devised that only *your* offer will do), but must *not* either hint or state that you're asking about *your* offer.

    d. Be ready to 'shift questions if his answers reveal that you were on the wrong track.

    e. Resume your questions, if he raises objections, as soon as you have handled them properly.

4. As he answers your questions, write down his answers, in a way I'll soon show. I suggest a *physical* technique like this one:

    a. Ask his permission to utilize any visual he has in the office, immediately get up to use it (without waiting for his permission) and employ it as I describe below.

    b. If he has no such visual, ask his permission to move around to his side, do so at once and let him see what I shall soon describe.

5. Now, here's how I suggest you write down his answers. Prepare (either at the visual or as soon as you have moved around to his side) a two-column spread like this:

6. As he answers one of your questions, write it down in the left-hand column. Leave enough space for what you are later going to write (regarding that answer) in the right-hand column and write down (in the left-hand column) the next answer, and so on, until you've asked all the questions you've intended to.

7. Now say to him: "I'm glad you've said what you did, because I have exactly what you need/want, and better than anyone else. Here, let me show you."

8. You now take each of his statements (in the left-hand column) and say: You said that you required. ... We offer that exactly as you stated it. Here, let me show you. You then write down briefly (talking as you write) your *proof* that that is so.

9. You do this in sequence until you've reached your last statement on the left.

10. Then you say: "Since we offer *exactly* what you need/want, ... " And you say or do what is necessary to get *him* to say or do what represents a firm commitment by him to accept *now* exactly what you've offered.

11. When you've gotten him to do that, you've accomplished your objective. Make whatever arrangements are necessary for follow-up and/or continuity, thank him and get out of there before he changes his mind.

FINALIZING STATEMENTS/ACTIONS

Before I begin to take up examples from my own experience with the question-close technique, it remains for me to suggest to you the more important statements and actions which you can employ (when you know he's ready for them) to get him to give you the firm commitment.

Objectives	Suggested finalizing questions/statements/actions
Acquaint the prospect with your company or its products or services.	What else can I tell you about us? What haven't I made as clear as I should have? Then I'm glad you know all about us and I'll be back to see you. ...
Get permission to bid.	What form or procedure do you want me to follow in submitting my bid? Thank you. How soon do you want it? You'll have it on time.
Get permission to help write specs.	When can my man come to see you to participate in the preparation of the specs? He'll be there.

Objectives	Suggested finalizing questions/statements/actions
Ascertain specs for a bid.	What are the specs? (Write them down unless they were handed to you.) Let me see if I've left anything out (understood you completely). What else do I need to know? Thank you. You'll have our bid on time and just as you want it.
Motivate a dealer/distributor to move your products/services more profitably.	What other facts would you like to have to convince you that it's to your best interest to sell ... units per ... of my product/service? Shall I send you ... units or ... units? Do you want Type A or Type B? Do you want them Monday or Tuesday? Shall I send them by truck or rail? Please check this order and see whether there's anything you'd like to add. Please sign here.
Get a dealer/distributor to use some/more of your advertising/promotion ideas/materials.	What additional facts do you wish in order to be convinced that my program is exactly what you need? When can you start— next week or two weeks from now? With whom shall I be working in your company? Which package do you want, this one or this one?
Get approval for working with his salesmen.	What else would you like to know about why it's to your best interests to let me work with your salesmen? How do you want to go about scheduling the visits? Whom shall I work with first? When will you want reports from me?
Get him to visit your plant.	Can you see how my product exactly fills your needs, or do you have to see it in operation first? If what I tell you turns out to be what I say, what do you know of that can do anywhere near as well? What day of the week is best for you? I'll be glad to stop by for you. What time is best? Whom would you like to take along with you?

Objectives	Suggested finalizing questions/statements/actions
Get his approval for a visit by my specialist.	How important is my proposed offer to you? Do you want the regular package or do you prefer to have a program tailored just for you? When can my man come and see you? To whom should he report? When can I come back to offer the tailored program?
Get him to test my offer.	On the face of it, how closely does my offer seem to meet your needs? What remains for you to be convinced to buy it at once? How soon can you test it? What shall I bring with me? Who'll be your liaison with me? How soon afterwards may I come for the report?
Get a firm order for a product/service.	Since I've been able to show you that what I'm offering meets your needs exactly, and better than anyone else can, which do you want to do, have me send in our purchase order form or use your own? Please initial this binder so I can earmark the items for you at once and not let my company give a priority to anyone else for it.
Satisfy a complaint.	What else do you want to bring to my attention about the way the item should function (is functioning)? Do you still have some dissatisfaction in mind or can I tell my people you're now entirely satisfied? When can I come back for a repeat order?

REAL-LIFE EXAMPLES

Now I'm going to take up a number of sales interviews made by salesmen with whom I went out on joint calls, in my capacity as sales consultant. Some of the situations I shall report will represent cases where the salesman did properly what I recommended. In others, I shall indicate how they should have performed. In all cases, I'll start with the planning stage, and, when we get to the call itself, move right into the step which immediately follows the model statement:

> Since I don't want to take up any of your or my time without great benefit to you, I must first find out exactly what your needs are and the extent to which my offer best meets them. In order to do that, I must ask you some questions. So, here goes.

Case Number 1.

PRODUCT/SERVICE: Spark plugs.

PROSPECT: Baking company.

OBJECTIVE: Prove that my plugs are better for his delivery trucks, so he will use them the next time he has to replace those now in the trucks.

My questions.	His answers.	How I handled each answer.
How often do you change plugs in a truck, on the average?	Once a year.	My plugs require an average change of once every 16 months. Here's the record for 12 of the leading deliverers of merchandise. I'd be glad to have you check with them.
How long does it take one of your mechanics to change a complete set of plugs?	Fifteen minutes.	Ours take no more that that at any time and often a little less. I'll be glad to have a few of your mechanics try it.
How much does it cost you annually per truck to change plugs, both labor and materials?	About $14.	Here are our proven statistics to show that with price and labor, over a three-year period, our expenses average only $11 a truck.
How much of a sup-	About 20 sets.	We have such

My questions.	His answers.	How I handled each answer.
ply do you have to keep on hand at all times?		prompt delivery service that you won't have to keep more than half that number on hand at any one time, which costs you less because you don't have to tie up the money involved.
When is the next time you will have to change a set of plugs?	Probably next week.	I'd like to leave these two sets of our plugs with you. Please use one of them at that time and the other the next time after that. I'll phone you next Friday to see how you made out and arrange to come by for a firm order, since I know how the test will come out.

Case Number 2.
PRODUCT/SERVICE: Brand-name eggs.
PROSPECT: Supermarket chain.
OBJECTIVE: Get them to put my eggs on their shelves for a period of two months and compare the rate of sale of my eggs with that of my competition.

My questions.	His answers.	How I handled each answer.
What brand of eggs do you now offer on your shelves?	Brands X and Y.	Those are good brands.

My questions.	His answers.	How I handled each answer.
What made you decide to carry those particular brands?	Our experience has shown that they have a good turn-over.	That's a good reason for carrying any reputable brand.
How many dozen per week do you sell, on the average, of Brand X, Brand Y—in an average store?	About 300 for Brand X and about the same for Brand Y.	That's not very much.
What's the average potential per store?	I don't really know.	Here are the figures for five of the leading supermarkets in your trade areas, compiled by the ABC Poll Co., showing that an average-sized chain like yours can sell 1,000 dozen eggs per week.
What figures have you seen on the sale of our brand?	None.	Here is our latest report from those same five chains, showing that we average 900 dozen per week in each of their stores of average size.
How many of your customers choose other stores in your areas because they want to do all their food shopping in one place and want our eggs?	I don't know.	Here are the results of a survey we made in three of your trade areas which show that you lose about 10% of your potential customers for that reason.
Why do you suppose more people want	I don't know. I suppose it has to do	Yes, our quality is better, and yes, they

My questions.	His answers.	How I handled each answer.
our eggs than those of Brand X or Y?	with better quality —but don't your eggs cost more?	cost a little more, but they still prefer them, not only because of the better taste and greater freshness but also because our packages are stronger and more attractive. Here—look and feel.
How much do you spend on promoting the purchase of those brands?	Well, the supplier shares half the cost.	We undertake the entire cost for promoting the purchase of our eggs in your stores. Here's a brochure explaining the program, which you can keep.

SEEKING A FIRM COMMITMENT:

Here's what I think you should do. You owe it to yourself to convince yourself that my brand is a must for you. I'd like to put sample stocking in any five stores you select, keep the statistics we always do, as explained in this sheet (which you can keep) and come back to you at the end of one month to compare notes with you. As soon as you approve the order for the volume of eggs involved in the samples, we'll start our advertising, promotion and merchandizing campaign—with your full knowledge and approval—and get the eggs into your stores at the right time. Now, here's our sample stocking order form, which I'll start filling out. What stores would you like to select? We generally recommend 50 dozen per store. Which of your stores do you think should have more than 50? Please sign here.

Case Number 3.
PRODUCT/SERVICE: Preparation of a catalogue for a company.
PROSPECT: A company which sells in the U.S. the products it imports from various parts of the world.
OBJECTIVE: Get him to budget for my kind of catalogue, tailored for his needs.

My questions.	His answers.	How I handled each answer.
How many different lines do you import?	About 20.	That's a large number of lines.
What geographical area do you cover in your sales promotion?	The entire U.S.	That's a big territory.
How do you now promote sales?	Through advertising in selected media.	That's good as a first step.
How many people write in asking for a description of your complete line?	About 1,000 a year.	That's a lot of people.
How do you answer their inquiries?	We write them back to ask them to be more specific in their inquiries, so we can give them only the important information.	That presents a few problems to my mind.
How much does it cost you to answer those inquiries that way?	About 50¢ an inquiry.	That's only an average cost for that kind of response.
What percentage of them write back with the details you want?	Only about 10%.	That's too high a loss of potential customers. Here are the national figures for sales in your kind of business, showing the per cent of purchase if they're answered completely, at once.
Why don't you answer their inqui-	We don't have a catalogue.	That may be a serious problem.

My questions.	His answers.	How I handled each answer.
ries by sending them your catalogue?		
If you had a catalogue, how much information could you put into it?	I guess enough to be able to answer all questions for all inquirers.	That would mean that all you'd have to do when you get an inquiry is send a cover letter, which can be an adapted form, and the catalogue.
How much are you prepared to spend on each inquiry doing it with a catalogue?	Well, I certainly would want it to be less than the 50¢ I'm now spending.	And you're absolutely right.
Who would be the man for me to work with to get the information I need for a proposal?	Why, you could work directly with me.	That's fine. Well, here's what I'm going to do.

SEEKING A FIRM COMMITMENT: I'll come in to see you with my graphic arts specialist. Will next Monday be better for you or do you prefer Tuesday? Fine! Ten a.m. or 2 p.m.? How many hours can you give us? Good! We'll draw from you all your specific needs for a catalogue and come back to you a week later with a firm proposal, which I know, from our past experience, will give you the best kind of promotion at considerably less than your present promotion costs.

Case Number 4.

PRODUCT/SERVICE: Metal display panels for helping to sell small manufactured appliances.

PROSPECT: A manufacturer of small electrical appliances who sells to distributors.

OBJECTIVE: To get him to place a trial order for 20 panels of a size fitting selected appliances, for experiment in each of his distributors' stores for the display of those appliances.

My questions.	His answers.	How I handled each answer.
How many distributors do you deal with?	Fifty.	That's a lot of outlets.
What products do you want them to sell for you?	All of my small appliances.	That makes for real economical marketing.
How satisfied are you with the volumes they sell?	Not at all. Some of them sell some of the appliances real well and neglect the others. Some don't sell any of them to my satisfaction.	That's what often happens with distributors.
How do your distributors promote your appliances to their customers?	Their customers come into the store, ask for what they want and buy whatever the salesman offers them, as long as it's what they need.	That seems o kind of hapnazar. approach.
What would you want your distributors to do about *your* appliances, as compared to those of your competitors?	Well, I'd like them to ask for *my* appliances by my company trade name.	That's exactly what we've got to get them to do.
What effect do you think it would have on your distributors' customers if they saw all your appliances attractively displayed, as soon as they approached the counter?	Well, it certainly could make them want to ask for *my* appliances.	That's right.

My questions.	His answers.	How I handled each answer.
How would you display all your appliances in any one store?	Why, I suppose I'd have to have some kind of board on which they'd all fit and which the distributor would want to display prominently.	I think you're on the right track.
What do you suppose would induce the distributor to display such a panel prominently?	Well, it would have to be convenient for him and the kind of thing he'd see as generally good for his store's image.	That's right, and that's exactly what I've got for you. Let me show you.

SEEKING A FIRM COMMITMENT:

Here is a photo of a typical products display panel of the kind we tailor for our many customers in related lines. Note how all the appliances fit neatly on the panel, how attractive the whole thing is and how suitable it is for the average store of the kind your distributors own. Now, I'll send our technical expert in to see you. He'll phone you tomorrow for an appointment. Then he'll tailor the kind of panel you need and show you all the samples and specs, for your approval, before we make them up especially for you, to your entire satisfaction. The price is $98 per panel in lots of ten panels, more expensive per panel if in smaller lots. Since you have 50 distributors, I suggest that a fair trial would be for 20. Then, if it turns out that you want certain modifications, we'll make the necessary adjustments and give you all 50 entirely as you need them. I've been writing this up as I talked. Please check this order and sign it here.

Case Number 5.

PRODUCT/SERVICE: Lightning-arresting system and equipment.

PROSPECT: City Purchasing Agent.

OBJECTIVE: To get him to visit our demonstration site, with his Chief Engineer, to see why he should buy my system.

My questions.	His answers.	How I handled each answer.
How many steel buildings and/or structures does the city operate?	Around 35.	That's just about the right number for us.
What kind of lightning-arresting systems do they now have?	Most of them don't have any and the rest use the XYZ system.	There's potential danger to your city in that setup.
What's the incidence of thunderstorms in your area?	Oh, during the hot months we get about five or six.	That's close to the national average.
How many times in the last year have buildings or structures of yours been hit by lightning?	About three.	That, too, is a fair average.
What did the total damage amount to?	About $100,000.	That's a lot.
Did any people get hurt, or were you lucky?	Three people were hurt, one seriously.	That's too bad.
At any one time, how many people could be in all of the buildings and structures?	Around 1,000.	That's a lot of people exposed to the possibility of lightning strikes.
Why don't you have effective lightning-arresters in all your buildings?	We haven't been satisfied with the ones we installed.	That's a good reason for not putting any more XYZ equipment in.
What do you want in	Something really	I'm glad that's what

My questions.	His answers.	How I handled each answer.
a lightning-arresting system?	effective, not too expensive and easy to maintain.	you want, because it's exactly what we have—the best on the market.
SEEKING A FIRM COMMITMENT:	You've got to see our system to believe it. We have an excellent setup in our nearby labs, which simulates lightning, of the kind your city gets. And, right on the spot, we have a few buildings with our system installed. The only way you will realize that our system is exactly what you need, and better than anything else anyone can produce, is to see it in action. And the only way to do that is to come to our lab in a very short time. You can't afford to delay it. We have two open dates within the next two weeks, April 15th and April 24th. Which date is best for you and your Chief Engineer to come there together? Good! I'll come by and pick you up here at 8 a.m. on the 15th. Thank you. I'll see you then.	

Case Number 6.

PRODUCT/SERVICE: Network radio advertising.

PROSPECT: Account Executive (for a popular soft drink) in an advertising agency.

OBJECTIVE: To get him to place a substantial part of his client's advertising budget, for the next three months, with my network.

My questions.	His answers.	How I handled each answer.
What is the total advertising budget of your client for the next three months?	Three million dollars.	That sounds like just about the right amount for their product.
How many people do they expect to reach effectively for that amount of money?	About 100,000.	With the right kind of coverage, they should have no problem.

My questions.	His answers.	How I handled each answer.
What statistics do you have on definite coverage for each type of medium you plan to use?	I haven't gotten into that yet.	Well, I have the latest reports on surveys made by the XYZ company, which I'll show you in a little while.
What geographical area do you want to reach with your advertising?	The metropolitan area.	That's good, because that's the scope of the survey I mentioned.
What age group do you want to reach?	Mostly the upper teens through the mid-thirties.	Good. My results cover the 18 to 34 age group.
What time of day are you planning to do the bulk of your radio advertising?	I hadn't decided that yet.	That's no problem. Our survey shows that 6 to 8 p.m. is the best time for that age group.

SEEKING A FIRM COMMITMENT:

Well, I'm glad we've agreed on most points. Here's the survey I talked to you about earlier. As you see, it shows conclusively that our network is number one among all the others in the metropolitan area in coverage for the 18-34 age group, which is the one you want to reach. And, as I said, the best time is 6 to 8 p.m. The survey goes on to show that we consistently reach over 100,000 young listeners during those hours. Therefore, we meet all of your requirements better than anyone else does, in any medium, and exactly as you stated them. There is, therefore, no need for you to devote more than one-third of your total budget for the next three months to anyone else but us. I'll draw up a complete, proposed schedule for you, tailored to your needs. When can I come back with it—Thursday of next week or Friday?

Summary

1. While your long-range objective for every call is to come away with an order, you can't always do so in each type of business.
2. Every call must, however, have a valid objective, and the achievement of that objective is the *close* of that call.
3. The use of questions will make it possible for you to detect signals, early in the interview and all along, which should tell you either to change your objective or leave that prospect to another time (or not at all), permitting you more time with other prospects more likely to let you win.
4. Your *close* activities begin just as soon as you are face to face with the prospect. Everything you do and say should lead, step by step, to a logical/chronological development in his mind that he must, at the end, do/say everything you want him to.
5. Unless the signals reveal that you're barking up the wrong tree, every new step you take brings him along steadily and surely to the right point, at which you must seek a firm commitment.
6. Then, at the right moment, you say/do the right thing to get him to commit himself, make any necessary arrangements for follow-up and get out of there. You've made it happen.

How to Handle Difficult Objections Boldly and Go in for a Sure Close with Effective Make-Happen Questions

WHAT IS AN OBJECTION?

An *objection* by a prospect is either a statement, a question, an action or a reaction by him—conscious or unconscious—to either:

- —Something *you* have said or done; or
- —Your very presence there, at least at that time and/or for the reason for that presence; or
- —You, your company and/or what you're trying to sell him; or
- —His own frame of mind, his emotional situation at the time, how he is feeling at that time and/or something that has happened or is happening to him, regardless of you; or
- —His relation to others in his own company; or
- —All salesmen; or
- —Any number of other things which make him unwilling to be receptive to you, your company, your presence there, what you have said/done (or are saying/doing) or what you want of him that day.

WHEN AND WHY AN OBJECTION IS RAISED

Objections are generally raised by prospects at any one or more of three times:

1. Toward the beginning of the interview, because the prospect doesn't really want to spend any time with you and will say or do anything to encourage you to leave and permit him to go on with his own plans.
2. Somewhere along the process of your presentation when he might have to admit to himself that what you have to offer him could be of benefit to him, but he doesn't want to give in, for whatever reason.

3. Anywhere during the interview, because either:

    a. He doesn't really understand something that you are saying or doing; or

    b. He doesn't agree with something you are saying; or

    c. He wants additional or different information; or

    d. He positively doesn't want to continue the conversation for any reason; or

    e. He's bored with you or what's going on; or

    f. You haven't succeeded in talking in terms of *his* interest; or

    g. You haven't really listened or responded to what *he* has said; or

    h. You haven't given him a chance to talk; or

    i. You have lost his attention; or

    j. He isn't willing or ready to make a decision; or

    k. He's definitely made up his mind not to go along with you on your objective.

HOW TO ANTICIPATE AND AVOID OBJECTIONS

Why is this important? Because:

- Objections can delay you in the progress of your sales development.
- They can interrupt the train of thought—yours as well as the prospect's—causing a failure to be as convincing as you might otherwise be.
- They can cement the prospect's resistance to your ideas.
- They can be an insurmountable obstacle to your goal.

Therefore, to the extent that you can avoid his raising objections, you eliminate those factors which might make your task more difficult if not impossible to achieve.

The bold anticipation and avoidance of objections are so closely intertwined that I might just as well treat them as one process.

Here's how I recommend you plan to anticipate and avoid the raising of objections by the prospect:

1. When you are planning your whole approach to the interview, think through all the possible reasons why the prospect might not want to do or say what you want him to.

2. Write these down on a separate sheet of paper.

3. As you write down your plan for what you are going to say and the questions you're going to ask during the sales call, keep that sheet of objections before you. Try to include in your statements/questions factors which will prevent him from thinking of objections because you either

have already included the answers to his anticipated questions or because your plan will make him realize how trivial and unimportant his objections might be.

Let's take an example.

The Case of the Plastic Bucket

I was working with a salesman whose company manufactured plastic buckets for a variety of containerizing needs. He was planning for the next day's call on a paint manufacturer who put his finished product out in quart-sized containers. The prospect was now using a metal bucket, and had been doing so for a long time. He had never used plastic buckets before. My salesman colleague had, as his objective for the call, to set up a trial run of the plastic bucket for the manufacturer.

Here's the list of objections we were able to come up with:

- The new line of plastic buckets would involve an inventory investment for him which he might not want to make.
- He might want to delay action on the new line until he discussed it with other suppliers of plastic buckets.
- He might want to discuss the new idea with other people in his company, despite the fact that he is authorized to make the decision himself.
- He would probably want a low-price contract before acceding to the trial run, with options to him.

In planning the call, we made sure to include—in the proper sequence of the development of the interview—the following questions/ statements, to be presented before he had a chance to raise any of those objections:

1. How much of an inventory do you now have of metal buckets?
2. How much do you think it will cost you to put in a supply for the test run? (Figures to show how little that would amount to.)
3. What problems are you now having with your metal buckets? (List of suggested problems to supplement his, if necessary.)
4. Who else makes plastic buckets besides us? What do you know about them? (Facts to show that they don't come anywhere near us.)
5. Who has authority to make this decision in your company? How much are you losing every day that you continue to use metal buckets? (Facts to show the true state of this loss, if necessary.)
6. What is it now costing you to put your paints into metal buckets? (Facts to supplement his, if necessary.)
7. What do you think it will cost you to make this trial run? (Figures showing

that you are already offering him a price appreciably lower than what he is now paying.)

THE QUESTION TECHNIQUE AS AN OBJECTION-AVOIDER

Aside from what I have said above, however, I must point out o you that the proper use of questions already has built into it the most effective avoidance of objections. Let me show you how and why questions make things happen to objections.

A. Instead of making statements, you ask questions. This prevents him from objecting to anything *you* have said because you haven't made any assertions.

B. His answers to your questions reveal to you how his mind is working, thus leading you to the next question/statement consistent with what he has just said. This, too, cuts down on the number of objections he might raise.

C. If your questions indicate that you're on the wrong track, you can try a different track, thus preventing him from raising objections stemming from your *being* on the wrong track.

D. When you finally get around to making statements, rather than asking questions, all you're doing is saying: "I'm glad *you* said you needed/ wanted. . . . That's exactly what I'm offering you, better than anyone else. Here, let me show you how."

This cuts down immeasurably on the possibility of his raising an objection.

HANDLING OBJECTIONS

However, for all of your efforts, a prospect here and there is bound to raise an objection now and then. When this comes about, you've got to handle it boldly or you might lose the game.

Here are some suggestions on the *timing* of your response to his objections. Later I'll talk about how best to handle them through the use of questions.

Early Objections

As I said before, the prospect is apt to raise feeble objections at the very outset, in order to discourage you from staying there. The thing to do under those circumstances is to show him courtesy but pooh-pooh the objection.

Here are some examples:

Objections	Suggested responses
I really don't have any time for you today. I have only a few minutes to spare for you.	That's fine. My time is limited, too. If I haven't got exactly what you need, it'll be obvious in a few minutes, and we can both take care of more important matters.
I'm not buying anything today. I have all I need.	That's okay. I'm not here to sell you anything today. All I want to do is lay the groundwork for our present or future relationship.

Then you go right on with your plan, unless, of course, he really means it, in which case he'll make it quite plain to you. In that latter case, you'd do best to plan on coming back when he's more receptive.

Mid-Stream Objections

Now let's talk about objections which he might raise anywhere along the path, where it's obvious he doesn't want to be convinced, at least not yet, because either:

- He doesn't want to seem an easy mark; or
- He doesn't feel like making a decision; or
- He's afraid to make a commitment.

My suggestion is that you handle these objections in a "yes, but" style. Here are some examples:

At one point in the conversation he says:	You can say:
You may be right. Why don't you leave a brochure and I'll let you know.	That's a good idea, and I shall leave one before I go, but, first I'd like to ask you another question. How frequently do you have to change your present . . .?
Sounds like a good idea, but I've already exhausted my current open-to-buy. I'll call you when I have more money available.	That's very kind of you. But, let me ask you this: How much business have you lost in the last six months by not carrying my line?

At one point in the conversation he says:	You can say:
I want to think about it.	Good. You do that. But, meanwhile, what are the factors you want to think about? Maybe I can cut down on the number of unknowns in your mind about how my service will benefit you.

Then you continue with your plan unless he is quite firm, in which case you approach his objection as a real one, and tackle it as recommended below.

MEETING THE REAL MCCOY

Now let's take up in detail how best to meet objections which are perfectly apparent as important, significant and unavoidable.

The first suggestion I have is that if one is raised at a time when you want to round out or complete a thought you're already embarked on, you say something like this:

"Yes. That's very important. Let me make a note of that." (Do so.) "I'll come back to that real soon." (Do so.) "But, now, I want to finish up what we were talking about." (Do so.)

If he doesn't go along with your wish for a delay, give in to him, handle the objection right then and there and, just as soon as possible, go back to what was going on before his interruption. Make sure to go back far enough to replace him in the proper frame of reference and continuity.

This brings us, then, to the best way of handling a serious or important objection when it is raised or when you are ready to tackle it. (Under no circumstances should you try to ignore it.)

Questions and Objections

The basic technique I recommend is:

- He says something or asks a question which amounts to a doubt, obstacle, disagreement, objection or other less-than-receptive attitude on his part toward what you are saying/doing.
- As he talks, listen very carefully (and watch, as appropriate) with an attentive, serious, neutral expression on your face and in your manner. Don't interrupt. Take notes if desirable.
- When he has finished, say something like this: "That's very interesting. Just what do you mean by . . . ?"—and you move right into the kind of question I describe below.

The whole concept I wish to discuss with you is this:

1. The vast majority of prospects desiring to raise an objection will not state it clearly, nor will they always state what's really bothering them. And they frequently mix several points into one statement—some important, others not.

2. If you respond to what they *say*, especially if you interpret what they say, you may be drawing the wrong inference, giving undue emphasis or strength to something they don't consider important and/or arguing about what they don't really have in mind.

3. Therefore, as soon as they say something that sounds like an objection, ask a question at once, which will force them to either:

   a. Say *exactly* what they mean; or
   b. Give specific details; or
   c. Distinguish between the important and the less so in what they've said.

4. Then you refrain from meeting "head on" what they first said and tackle: what they *really* mean; the *exact* meanings they intend for the words they use; the specifics rather than the generic complaint.

5. In this way, you can either overcome the objection or realize that there's no point in pursuing that track at that time.

EXAMPLES

Now I'm going to take a number of objections that have been raised in my presence, during joint calls, and describe how they either *were* handled or should have been.

Situation Number 1.

Offering: A dairy product, to a supermarket buyer.

Objective: Get him to stock my product in his dairy case.

Objection: He has only limited space in his case and can't make room in it for my product.

Attack: 1. What criteria do you use for allotting space in your case? (Mostly the greater profit to me or the proven demands of the customers.)

2. Approximately how many demands do you get for these other products in the case?

3. What's your percentage of markup on each of those products?

4. Here are validated statistics, prepared by the leading survey company in your field, showing that:

   a. Our product has this proportion of demand over the kinds of products you stock here: . . . .

          b. Our product sells . . .% more than these others.

     5. Here are our figures for the last two years, and our projection for the year we're now in, showing that your markup with us is greater than with the others: . . . .

Situation Number 2.

Offering: A medication (non-prescription), to a drugstore.

Objective: Get the owner to buy three cases now and promote their sale to his patrons.

Objection: Your product has not been sufficiently exposed to the consumer to attract his coming here to ask for it, or, once here, to want it.

Attack: 1. What criteria do you use for exposure?

              2. Here's a record of our promotion campaign, with the accompanying statistics, to show that we amply meet your criteria.

Situation Number 3.

Offering: Radio advertising time for a tourist attraction.

Objective: Get the time-buyer to give me an order for a trial announcement series.

Objection: He personally doesn't like the kind of music my station plays and therefore thinks that very few people tune in on my station.

Attack: 1. What kinds of people generally come to see your attraction? (Economic class; ages; sex predominance, if any; educational background; profession/occupation.)

              2. Additionally, what kinds of people does he want to attract who are not now visiting his establishment?

              3. Here are figures to show that . . . people of these categories . . . regularly listen to our programs.

              4. I don't question the good taste you show in your musical preferences, but our station reaches the very people you want to tell about your place.

Situation Number 4.

Offering: Review books for students in a school system, to the system's purchasing agent for books.

Objective: Get him to order now (in the spring) the books he'll need in the fall.

Objection: A new line of review books published by a competitor is coming out two weeks before the new school year starts, and he wants to try it out.

Attack: 1. How many of the new books have you examined?

              2. We've compared them to ours and have discovered the following superiorities for *you* of ours over theirs: . . . . .

3. Why don't you try only a limited number of their books and use ours, which have given you such consistent satisfaction?

4. What assurance do you have that they'll be able to deliver the books on time with such a late publication date?

Situation Number 5.

Offering: A sampling service for a cosmetics manufacturer's secondary product line.

Objective: To get the manufacturer to let us tailor a program for that secondary line in order to promote it without interfering with the highly profitable sale of his primary line.

Objection: My price is too high.

Attack: 1. That's an important point. But, when you say that my price is too high, I'm not entirely clear on what you mean, exactly.

2. Too high for what?

3. What's the relation between the price I'm asking and the profits I can assure you as a result of my program?

4. Look at these figures and you'll see that for every dollar you spend on my program, you get a net profit of . . . dollars: . . . .

Situation Number 6.

Offering: Special hardware to the senior buyer of a company that manufactures vending machines.

Objective: To get him to buy my hardware.

Objection: He now manufactures, himself, the parts I want him to buy from me.

Attack: 1. What does it cost you to manufacture those parts by yourself? (Here are my figures to show you that while our initial price is higher than your cost, in the long run it costs you less.)

2. What is the schedule of your ability to manufacture those parts to meet your needs? (Here are my figures to show that I can always meet your schedules much more efficiently than you can.)

3. How much space and money do you have to devote to keeping the kinds of inventories you need on hand? (Here are the figures to show that we can keep all the parts you need at no cost to you.)

4. What problems do you have in getting and keeping the labor you need for making those parts? (Why not concentrate on the labor problems of the manufacture for which you are in business? We have no labor problems. Here's the proof: . .)

5. What problems have you had with the quality of the parts you make? (We've mastered those problems because of our specialization.)

Situation Number 7.

Offering: Dry-bulk shipping containers, to a large trucking company.

Objective: To get the buyer to run a trial with my containers.

Objection: I'm entirely satisfied with the containers I'm now using.

Attack:
1. That's a very understandable situation to be in if you really have no reason for questioning your degree of being satisfied.
2. I would be remiss if I didn't question it, which is why I'm going to ask you some questions.
3. Which of these benefits do you derive from your present containers?
   a. Absolute prevention of leakage. (Ours is a sealed, vacuum-flow system.)
   b. Minimum contamination. (Ours is zero.)
   c. Ease of cleaning liner. (Ours is easiest to clean because of the nature of the plastic used.)
   d. Minimum of customer damage claims. (Here's the record among our customers: . . . .)
   e. Minimum maintenance cost. (Here are our figures: . . . . . .)
   f. Minimum operating costs. (Here are our figures: . . . . . .)
   g. Customer acceptance. (Here are some testimonials from your own customers who have used other services employing our containers: . . . .)
4. What is your present degree of satisfaction with your current containers?

Situation Number 8.

Offering: Coffee for an airline.

Objective: To get the senior buyer to negotiate a contract with my company for his line's coffee commitments.

Objection: I've been dealing with your competitor for the last 20 years, and I have a strong sense of loyalty to him because of the way he has dealt with us all that time.

Attack:
1. Loyalty's a fine quality, but in business, which is more important to you—the best possible coffee contract for your company or a sense of loyalty unrelated to profit?
2. Let's see whether your loyalty to him is more important to you than the degree to which my contract can benefit you.
   a. Taste the difference between the two coffees. Which do *you* like better?

    b. Why isn't your airline on this list of the best-tasting coffee-servers among all the lines?

    c. How long does it take to prepare your present coffee? (Ours seeps through more quickly.)

    d. What kind of cooperative advertising does your present supplier offer you? (Look at our program.)

    e. How does his packaging compare to this?

3. All around, what's your loyalty to the other supplier costing you, as compared to the profitability of using our coffee?

Situation Number 9.

Offering:	Automotive parts, to a parts dealer.
Objective:	Get an order for my parts.
Objection:	Business is bad right now.
Attack:	1. Why is business bad for you?
	2. What kinds of customers aren't coming in that used to?
	3. Why aren't they coming in?
	4. How come the stores that are handling my products in your city are doing a good business?

Situation Number 10.

Offering:	An epoxy sealant, to a company which uses our coatings.
Objective:	To get the company to use the sealant on those coatings.
Objection:	The buyer is afraid that the sealant might adversely affect the kind of finish he puts on the coating.
Attack:	1. What kind of adverse effect are you talking about?
	2. When and under what circumstances has this kind of sealant had that effect on the coating?
	3. What other factors might have entered into the situation you describe?

Situation Number 11.

Offering:	Culvert pipe, to the Chief Engineer of a state.
Objective:	To get him to approve my pipe for use in state culverts.
Objection:	My pipe doesn't meet the state's requirements/specs.
Attack:	1. In what respects do we fail to meet those specs?
	2. Where have you tried our pipe out?
	3. What results do you get from our competitor's pipe in those areas? (Here is proof that the strong acid conditions in those areas are causing the same damage to our competitor's pipe as to ours: . . . .)
	4. In what other respects do we fail to meet your specs? (None.)

Situation Number 12.

Offering:	A new catalyst, to a chemical manufacturer.
Objective:	To get him to test a sample.
Objection:	Since your product is brand new, it has no proven commercial history of superiority for us. We can't afford to try out unproven products.
Attack:	1. How much will it cost you to test a sample?
	2. How great a risk to your profit does that involve?
	3. What do you think are the profits to be gained from the use of my new catalyst?
	4. How does that compare with the cost of testing the sample?

Situation Number 13.

Offering:	Exclusive service of temporary employees, to a large employer of office girls.
Objective:	To get him to use only my service when he needs temporaries.
Objection:	Your service isn't any better than the competition's, so I'd just as soon spread it around.
Attack:	1. If it were true that we were no better, in any respect, than our competitors, I'd go along with you.
	2. But there are a number of respects in which they can't come anywhere near us, and I'd like to take them up one at a time.
	3. First, let's talk about insurance.
	a. What kind of insurance does our competition offer to cover your liability regarding the temporaries?
	b. How does that compare with ours, which is: . . . . . . ?
	c. What happens if you hire some girls from our competition and you incur a liability which they don't cover the way we do?
	4. Now let's talk about the second way in which our superiority to our competition makes it absolutely unwise for you to deal with anyone else but us: . . . .

Situation Number 14.

Offering:	Air travel incentive programs (foreign company) for a company's sales force.
Objective:	To get them to offer our programs for sales-contest prizes.
Objection:	You are a foreign company. I want to buy American.
Attack:	1. What competitive incentive programs are you now using?
	2. How do they compare in their attractiveness, motivation and cost to *our* programs?

3. How much money do you suppose my company spends in the United States? (Show how a large percentage of the profits of the foreign airline is spent here.)

Situation Number 15.

Offering:	Yarn pressroom products, to a distributor.
Objective:	To get him to carry my line.
Objection:	He has been burned before, by companies making the same claims as mine has.
Attack:	1. Precisely what claims did they make that you got burned on?
	2. Why do you assume that we will burn you in the same way?
	3. How many of these satisfied customers do you know?
	4. In order to find out how we backed up our claims to them, do you want to phone them yourself, or would you like me to do it for you right now?

Situation Number 16.

Offering:	Cutlery, to a distributor.
Objective:	To get him to carry my line in his stores.
Objection:	The markup on my cutlery isn't as high as it is on my competitor's.
Attack:	1. What markup do you have on the competitive line?
	2. What gross margin does that give you per item?
	3. What's the average volume of sales of that line per month?
	4. What's the total gross margin per month?
	5. Now look at these figures: Average volume in comparable stores, . . . Times gross margin per item, ... Total gross margin, ...

OBJECTIONS AND THE MAKE-HAPPEN CLOSE

Now let's discuss the last point outlined in the beginning of this chapter. How can you go right into the close after you have successfully handled the prospect's objections?

Let's review, first, the sequence of steps I recommend for this part of the interview.

Initial Closing Attempt

You will recall that, in previous chapters, I suggested you make things happen as follows:

1. You've asked all the questions you intended to.
2. The prospect has answered them by telling you that he needs/wants a

specific *something,* you not having mentioned *your* objective or product/service yet.

3. You then take up each point he has raised, which is best met by what *you* have to offer, and say:

    a. I'm glad you said that you need/want. . . .

    b. That's exactly what I have to offer. Here, let me show you what I have for meeting that precise need/want: . . . .

    c. Here's how what I have to offer meets what you said you needed/wanted.

    d. Here's the proof that it's better than anything else you can possibly use for that purpose.

4. You then—immediately—say/do something calculated to get him to make a firm commitment—*now*—to what you want him to accept from you.

This last step is your first attempted close. If he accepts your offer at that time, you immediately move into the statement or action (or both) by him, representing your achievement of your objective for that call, and (after making follow-up arrangements) skedaddle right out of there.

Objections and Closing Attempt(s).

Suppose, however, he raises an objection—the valid kind—somewhere along the line. How does this affect your closing attempts?

This is best treated in two separate types of situations:

- *The objection is raised before your first attempted close.* You handle the objection (unless you can properly postpone it), review the necessary number of steps that preceded the objection and go on from there as though the objection had never been raised (except that you incorporate into your next steps whatever you may have learned from his objection).
- *The objection is raised right after your first attempted close.* This is the type I want to develop in detail now.

Rationale

Here's how I suggest you function in that kind of situation:

1. You've tried to close.
2. He says something like: "Hey, wait a minute! Not so fast! I'm not ready for that yet."
3. He then raises his objection.
4. You handle it effectively at once.
5. You immediately move right in again for the close, with either the same ploy as before, or, if the objection warrants, a different ploy.
6. If he raises the same objection again (in the same or different way), or a different objection, you handle that and again move right into the close.

7. If you can't get him to commit himself, no matter what you do or say (after a reasonable number of attempts), leave the door open for coming back later under more favorable circumstances (or start on a new objective with him) and beat it gracefully. As soon as possible after that, when there are no prospects to be seen, analyze why you failed and take appropriate corrective steps regarding him or anybody else.

8. If you close, make necessary arrangements for follow-up and scram.

EXAMPLES

Now let's take up some actual situations I've experienced where a salesman acted properly in trying to close immediately after handling objections.

Example Number One.

Product/service: Food acidulant.

Prospect: Chain of supermarkets.

Objective: To get them to convert from citric acid to a fumaric acid.

Objection raised: This would require a changeover by us of production procedures.

How handled: 1. How long do you think it would take to make the changeover? (It's agreed that this is a minimal time.)
2. What will be the *net* increase of profits after the changeover? (It's agreed that this will be considerable.)

Re-close: Then I'll send the first shipment to you at once. Do you want it by United Parcel Service or would you rather we deliver it in our own truck?

Example Number Two.

Product/service: Light farm equipment.

Prospect: Farm machine and equipment dealer.

Objective: To get him to carry my line.

Objection raised: I don't have enough money to finance the purchase of your equipment.

How handled: 1. How much money do you think it would take for the kind of initial order we've agreed on?
2. How would it help if I offered you these terms: . . . ? (Agreed that he could manage it.)

Re-close: As you were indicating the conditions under which you could afford to introduce this line, I've been making notes on our order form. Please look at it to make sure it says exactly what you agreed to and sign it here.

Example Number Three.

Product/service: Shoestring potatoes.

Prospect: Food store.

Objective: To get them to stock and display these snack items.

Objection raised: I already have too many snack items.

How handled: 1. What's your goal in handling any one snack item?

2. Which of your current items are consistently meeting those goals?

3. Which of them meet your goal as consistently and as well as my snack item does in comparable stores, according to these figures?

Re-close: So I suggest that you replace one or more of the less-desirable snack items you're now carrying with mine. As a trial run, I'm putting you down for the minimum stock we recommend for all new customers. Do you want these in your hands by the beginning or the middle of next week?

Example Number Four.

Product/service: Fleet-vehicle leasing.

Prospect: Chain of florists.

Objective: To get them to contract for leasing their delivery vans from us.

Objection raised: I *own* everything in my business and don't want to depart from that policy.

How handled: 1. When you lease vehicles from us, what *debt* do you incur that is in any way different from what you owe on merchandise you buy?

2. How important to you is an abstract concept in the face of the proven superiority to you of leasing over owning your own vans?

Re-close: Please examine this contract now, in the light of what we've just discussed, and initial it here.

Example Number Five.

Product/service: Electric heating system.

Prospect: Construction company.

Objective: To get them to try our system in a new house they're putting up.

Objection raised: The public doesn't accept the advantage to them of that kind of system in a house.

How handled: 1. What makes you say that?

2. What public are you talking about?

3. Where did you get that information?

4. How does that compare with these statistics I have here?

Re-close: I'm ready to submit complete plans for the system in your new house. With whom shall I work?

Example Number Six.

Product/service: Table saw.

Prospect: Cabinet maker.

Objective: To sell him the saw.

Objection raised: I don't have any job now, or in the offing, big enough to warrant a saw of this size.

How handled: 1. How do you get customers?

2. Why don't you get jobs big enough for this kind of saw?

3. How much of this big-job market in your area (shown by these figures of mine) are you failing to tap because they know you don't have this kind of saw?

Re-close: You can buy this saw on a one-year payment plan, or you can get a 10% discount on payment in full within 30 days. Which way do you want to pay for it?

Example Number Seven.

Product/service: A credit-management service.

Prospect: Hospital.

Objective: To get them to engage my company to manage their credit system.

Objection raised: We run this hospital as a service to the community. It's not a profit-making business. We aren't geared for that kind of efficiency.

How handled: 1. How much of a deficit do you have each year?

2. How much of that comes from credit losses?

3. How easy is it for you to get all the money you need for your budget?

Re-close: Whom shall we contact in your organization to install the system?

Example Number Eight.

Product/service: A liqueur.

Prospect: Liquor store.

Objective: To get approval for a new freight routing.

Objection raised: The new routing will eliminate my ability to take advantage of pool shipments, and this will mean that I'll have to order more cases at one time than I need.

How handled: 1. How much does it cost you to increase your inventory under the new routing?

2. How much will you save by the new routing?

3. In the long run, which routing costs you less?

Re-close: We can start the new routing with your next order. I've put you down for 20 cases. Please see whether I have all the details correct on this form and initial it here.

Example Number Nine.

Product/service: Liquid fertilizer for an irrigation system.

Prospect: Ranch owner.

Objective: To sell him a tank for the storage and delivery to his fields of my liquid fertilizer.

Objection raised: Neither I nor my people know how to use or measure liquid fertilizers.

How handled: 1. Who's in charge of storing and distributing the fertilizer you're now using?
2. How soon can I start training him in the new system?
3. How shall I contact him?

Re-close: What time of day or evening is best for you to have us deliver and install the tank? . . . . We'll have it here on Wednesday of next week.. Is that all right, or would you prefer Thursday?

Example Number Ten.

Product/service: Pension plan.

Prospect: Commercial company.

Objective: To introduce new enrollment procedures.

Objection raised: The Internal Revenue Service won't approve of the new procedure.

How handled: 1. What makes you say that?
2. What aspects of the new procedure do you think they won't approve?
3. What sections of the law say that?
4. Can you point to the section(s) in this booklet?

Re-close:When do you want to install the new procedure, at the beginning of the new quarter or before you prepare your next payroll?

Example Number Eleven.

Product/service: Natural gas.

Prospect: Manufacturing company.

Objective: To get them to change their supplier and buy it from me.

Objection raised: Natural gas is natural gas. What difference does it make whom I buy it from?

How handled: 1. What do you look for in a supplier?
2. What's the importance to you of service?
3. How important is it to you to have your supplier's representative call on you frequently to avoid or solve problems?
4. What kind of help do you need in maintaining your equipment?

Re-close: We have installation time available this week and next week. After that, we're solidly booked for a few weeks. If I send our man in on Friday of this week, what time of morning can he start?

Example Number Twelve.

Product/service: Lighting to prevent burglaries.

Prospect: Club having its own meeting and headquarters building.

Objective: To present the benefits of their using my lighting system (for the prevention of burglaries) to their members, at their next meeting.

Objection raised: We already have a full agenda for our next meeting and can't possibly make time for you.

How handled: 1. When is the meeting after that?

2. How many nights of additional opportunities for break-ins does that offer to the many criminals in your area?

3. Can this issue be resolved without the approval of the membership?

4. Which of the items of your present agenda could you shorten in order to give me the ten minutes I need?

Re-close: Why don't you put me on at this point in the agenda? As I see it, the members will welcome it. Let's look at your electrical outlets so I can plan the equipment I need to bring along for my audio-visual aids.

Example Number Thirteen.

Product/service: Paints.

Prospect: Distributor.

Objective: To have him stock my line.

Objection raised: I don't have a warehouse as close to his store as that of his present supplier.

How handled: 1. What advantage does that closeness bring to you?

2. What do you require by way of delivery and service?

3. What do you require that isn't already provided for you in this plan of mine? . . . .

Re-close: I've put you down for our usual initial order for a store like yours. Please sign here.

Example Number Fourteen.

Product/service: Cushioning material for packing.

Prospect: Manufacturer.

Objective: To get him to try our material in a test run.

Objection raised: Our quality assurance people have found materials like yours unsatisfactory.

How handled: 1. What specific materials have they tried and rejected?

2. What aspects of those materials have they rejected?

3. Please compare the specs of my materials with those of the ones rejected. Which of my specs are acceptable under your standards? Can you point to any of my specs which are unacceptable, or is it true that there are none?

Re-close: When can we make this test run? Can you manage it this week or will next week be better for you?

Summary

1. An objection can be expressed or implied, but the salesman must know when it has been raised.
2. An objection can be a question, an obstacle, an attitude, a statement or a gesture.
3. A prospect has a variety of reasons for raising objections, but they generally fall into three basic categories:

    a. Those raised very early in the interview, in the hopes that the prospect won't have to spend time he doesn't really want to.
    b. Those intended to avoid the necessity of the prospect giving in to a logical presentation because he isn't ready or willing to make a decision.
    c. Those which are really valid.

4. The best thing to do with objections is to try to anticipate them and, therefore, prevent their being raised, because they:

    a. Take up valuable time.
    b. Tend to set up undesirable attitudes.
    c. Interrupt the logical and chronological flow of ideas.

5. Through the proper planning and use of questions, most objections can be avoided.
6. When a less valid objection is raised, the salesman should try to bypass it.
7. When a valid objection is raised, the salesman should:

    a. Ask questions in order to determine the real objection behind the words used.
    b. Attack that real objection and disregard the original expression.

8. If an objection has been raised during the presentation, before the salesman is ready to close, the salesman should (if he can't avoid handling it at that time), as soon as ' he has overcome the objection, review a few steps before the objection was raised and continue on from there right to the close.
9. If an objection is raised right after the salesman's attempt to close, the salesman should:

    a. Handle the objection.
    b. Immediately try to close again.

INDEX

A

Advertising, 66
Aluminum castings, 42-50
    interview,
        objective, 44
    question guide, 48-51
    quote, 44
Attention, 88, 89
    attracting, 88
    and interview, 88
    keeping, 88, 92
    questions for getting, 89, 103-110

B

Banana ripening process, 23
Beginning to close:
    the commitment, 184
    the objective, 184
Benefits, 89
Bids, 65
    piping, 83, 84

C

Catalogue preparation, 194-196
Catering service:
    prospecting, 82, 83
Cereal, 28-33
Chemicals, 75
Close:
    continuing process, 28, 186
    failure, 184
    finalizing statements/actions, 188-190
    firm commitment, 134
    and objections, 216-223
    the make happen, 134
    partitions, pre-fabricated, 19
    and prospect's decision, 16
    psychology of, 134
    and questions, 185-188
    questions, technique, 186-188
    reasons for question technique, 35, 36
    and sales, 18
    the signed order, 134
    steps to, 28-33
Close-expediters, 185

C (continued)

Closing:
    definite, 27, 28
Commitment, 66, 159
Common Sense, 116
Complaint, handling,
    desks, 80
Convention facilities, 74, 75

D

Dealer:
    motivating the, 66
Dealer and salesmen:
    working with, 66
Designing questions, 67
Desks, 80
Display panels, 196-198

E

Eggs, 192
Electronics, 103
Emotions, role of, 144, 145

F

Fact:
    defined, 140
Fact, opinion or faith, 115, 116
    how to prove, 142, 143
    and demonstrations, 142, 143
    and reasoning, 144
    presentation, 141
Fasteners, 103
Follow-up, 66, 136
    paint, 81-82

G

Generalization:
    example, 115
Goal:
    the switch, 19, 20, 21
    illustration, 42
    preparation for, 42
    reason, pre-set, 42
    of sales calls, 182

H

Handguns, industrial, 70-71
Heavy equipment distributor, 67-69
Human behavior:
    and psychology, 114, 116
    and stimulus response, 116, 117

I

Industrial fasteners, 77, 78
Initiating the close, 186
Insurance, 51-59, 165-167
    interview, planning, 56-59
    worksheet, 52-59
Interest:
    benefits to prospect, 89
    how to maintain, 93-101
Intermediate objectives, 65, 67
Interruptions:
    how to handle, 88, 89
Interview:
    and attention, 88
    examples, 190
    finding the best objective, 65
    finding the right prospect, 65, 151, 152
    goal, 18
    how to handle objections, 207-210
    idea sequence, 18
    and interruptions, 88
    maintaining interest, 92-101
    objective, 44
    opening, 89, 90
    philosophy of closing, 135
    planning form, 43-47
    planning the objective, 64
    prospect,
        final steps, 51
    prospect,
        planning form, 43-47
    reasons for failure, 184
    and signal alertness, 185
    and small talk, 90
Interview time, 185

L

Lightning arresting system and equipment, 198-
    200
Logic:
    basic premise, 147-148
    close, 150
    examples, 147-161
    facets, 145

Logic *(cont.)*
    and questions, 146-161
    and questions,
        effective use, 146
    and reason, 145
    sales situations, 147
    in seeing more than one person, 152, 153
    seeing the right person, 152
Lumber, 76, 77

K

Key words:
    "above average," 172, 173
    "acceptance," 168, 169
    "afford," 174
    "availability," 171
    "cheaper," 167
    "closer," 175
    "committed," 177
    "competitive," 167, 168
    "create a need," 167
    "customer oriented," 169
    "durable," 175, 176
    "exclusive territory," 175
    "expertise," 176
    "get approval," 177, 178
    "limited distribution," 170
    "loyalty," 176, 177
    "more complete line," 169, 170
    "problems," 177
    "production," 178
    "profit," 173, 174
    "prompt delivery," 168
    "quality," 168
    "reliable," 169
    "same or similar," 171
    "to your satisfaction," 168
    "in stock," 176
    "support," 170, 171

M

Magic Question Technique:
    and the close, 28
Mailing brochures, 72-74
Make-Happen questions:
    and statements, 18
Motivating dealers, 66

O

Objections:
    and the close, 216-223

Objections *(cont.)*
    defined, 204
    examples, 210-216
    how to anticipate, 205, 206
    how to avoid, 205, 206
    how to handle, 135, 136, 207-209
    prevention, 135
    and questions, 209, 210
    valid, 209
    when raised, 204
    and close, 64
        commitment, 64, 159
    approval to work with salesmen, 158
    to arrange plant visits, 158
    to arrange for prospect needs, 159
    to arrange test, 158, 159
    to bid, 155
        or test progress, 159
    to bring in specialist, 158
    the commitment, 159
    establishing, 67
    expansion of sales, 150, 151
    to find the best goal, 153
    finding out specs, 156, 157
    firm commitment, 63, 64
    follow-up, 159, 160
    goal for sales contact, 64
    intermediate, 62-65
        introducing yourself, 65
    to maintain contact, 153, 160
    to motivate dealers, 157
    precise and alternative, 67
    to prepare for future call, 154
    prospects:
        importance, 62
        priorities, 62
        qualification, 62, 151, 152
        number of, 62
    qualifying the prospect, 151, 152
    quota, 63
    recommendations, 160, 161
    to satisfy complaint, 160
    satisfying the prospect, 63
    seeing the right person, 65, 152, 153
    selling the prospect, 62
    success in, 64
    ultimate, 62, 63
        questions, planning, 63
    sale, 63
    to use promotional materials, 157
    to write specs, 155
Office equipment, 84, 85
Office services, 76

Openers:
    first call, 90
    and questions, 90
    and rapport, 91, 92
    subsequent calls, 91
Order-taking, 141

P

Packaging, 69, 70
Paint, 81, 82
Philosophy of closing, 135
Piping, 83, 84
Plastic buckets, 206, 207
Planning:
    objective, 60
    review of records, 60
    effective, 60
Practice (application), 116
Premise:
    and development, 150-161
Presentation, 65, 122, 123
    effective, 65
    and rapport, 123
    and the superiority complex, 123
    and true selling situation, 122, 123
Probing, 65
Product, tailoring, 66
Programming, 77
Progress information, 66
Promotions:
    use of, 66
Prospect:
    advance information, 40-42
        sources, 41, 42
Prospects:
    characteristics of, 124
        how to handle, 123, 124
    conclusions, 63
    convincing the, 26
    facts presentation, 141
    formulating questions, 47
    gaining the objective, 67
    how to maintain interest, 89, 93-101
    introduction, 65
    involvement, 23, 24, 25
    maximum, 62
    needs, 16
    plans, 42, 44-47
    qualifying, 65
    reaction to salesman, 123
    and reasoning, 145
    seeing the right person, 65
    selling himself, 25, 26

Prospect interview:
    planning form, 43
Psychological principles, 117
Psychologist:
    how he arrives at a theory, 117
    how he functions, 117
Psychology:
    application, 118
        examples, 118-122
    and the close, 134
    defined, 114
    of the follow-up, 136
    generalization, 115
        example, 115
    in selling, 116, 118-122
    and stimulus response, 116, 117
    the study or art of human behavior, 114
    terms defined, 114-116
    theory, 114, 115
Psychology of objections, 135
    reasons for, 212, 135
Psychology of proof, 133
    clincher, 134
    rationale, 133
Psychology of questions, 125, 133
    in abrasives, 130, 131
    and communication, 125
    in computer-controlled inventory
        systems, 132
    in credit and collections, 131
    examples, 125-133
    in hiring, 133
    response, meaning, 125
    sales situations, 125-133
    in servicing fire extinguishers, 132
    in trucking, 130

Q

Question guide, 48-51
    for aluminum castings, 48-51
    for insurance, 52-59
Questions:
    for attention getting, 102-110
    magic, 19
    and objections, 209
    preparation, 47
    pre-planned, 186
    and response, 60
    used to maintain interest, 94
Question technique:
    and the close, 184
    as objection avoider, 207

R

Radiating antennas, 71, 72
Reasoning:
    and demonstration, 145
    and intellect, 145
    and logic, 144
Re-sale potential, 66
Review:
    of closing technique, 184-188
    of steps to sales, 182-184
Role of emotions, 144, 145

S

Sales successful, 63
    introduction, 90
    and semantics, 164-179
Sales calls:
    customer and prospect, 40
    preparation, 40-60
        examples, 42-59
    and the prospect, 41-42
Sales closes, 16
Sales consulting service, 20
Sales interview:
    reasoning, 21
    retaining interest, 22
Sales pitch, 17
Sales presentation:
    and logic, 146-161
Sales-training program, 20, 21
Selling:
    ability, 164, 165
    agricultural products, 79, 80
    aluminum castings, 42-50
    antenna systems, 71, 72
    banana ripening process, 23
    catalogue preparation, 194-196
    cereal, 28-33
    chemicals, 75
    convention facilities, 74, 75
    display panels, 196-198
    eggs, 192
    and emotions, 144
    follow-up, 66
    heavy equipment, 67-69
    industrial fasteners, 77, 78, 103
    industrial handguns, 70, 71
    lightning arresting system and equipment,
        198-200
    and logic, 140
    lumber, 76, 77
    mailing brochures, 72-74
    maintaining rapport, 66

Selling *(cont.)*

    network radio advertising, 200, 201

    office equipment, 84, 85

        and layout, 84, 85

    office services, 75, 76

    packaging, 69, 70

    plastic buckets, 206, 207

    programming, 77

    proving facts, 141-144

    and psychology, 116

    recommendations, 67

    and semantics, 164, 165

    service, 17, 18

    smoking urns, 78, 79

    spark plugs, 191, 192

    and stimulus response, 116, 117

    steel, 147-150

    thread, 17

    tractors, 67-69

    traditional approach, 27, 28

Selling steps, 118-122

    appointment, 120

    avoiding diversions, 122

    maintaining attention, 122

    maintaining rapport, 121

    firm objective, 119

    the physical situation, 121

    planning the interview, 119

    sales kit, 119

    seeing the right person, 120

    sticking to objective, 122

Semantic accuracy, 165-167

Semantics:

    defined, 164

    and key words, 167

    problems and solutions, 167-171, 172

    and questions, 165

    and sales, 164-179

Signal-alerters, 185

    and question technique, 185

Signals:

    hostile, 185

    in interview, 185

Signals *(cont.)*

    lack of conviction, 185

    lack of interest, 185

    lack of receptivity, 185

Small talk, 90

Smoking urns, 78, 79

Spark plugs, 192

Specialist and visits, 66

Specifications, (see Specs)

Specs, 65, 66

Statements:

    and questions, 18

Steel, 33-35 147, 148

Success:

    achieving, 182

    and effective planning, 183, 184

    and preparation, 183

    and time, 182, 183

Supermarket:

    waste removal, 85

Survey, 66

T

Technique:

    of beginning the close, 184

    of question asking, 182-184

Television advertising, 22, 23

Testing your product, 66

Time, value, 18

Theory:

    application, 117

    how it is validated, 117

Thread, 17

Tool distributor, 70, 71

Tractors, 67-69

W

Waste removal:

    supermarket, 85

Words, key, 165-178

Worksheet:

    close through questions, 43, 60